The Jesus Christ Papers

Volume 1

The Many Witnesses that "He lives!"

Richard W. Linford

The Jesus Christ Papers

Volume 1

The Many Witnesses that "He lives!"

A Sweetwater Book Company publication

First edition

ISBN 1-57574-021-4

Imprint Linford Corporation

Sold world-wide by www.Amazon.com

In 1986 I wrote and compiled an article about the witnesses who testify that Jesus Christ lives. That article was published in a Deseret News, LDS Church News center section, Week Beginning March 23, 1986, pp. 8-9. I have since come to appreciate the fact that although testimonies of witnesses bolster our faith that Jesus Christ lives, only by the witness of The Holy Spirit can we know Jesus is the Christ, the Son of the Living God. By the power of the Spirit we know He is Jehovah, The Messiah, The Living Christ and The Savior of the world. In the words of Paul:

1. And I, brethren, when I came to you, came not with excellency of speech or of wisdom, declaring unto you the testimony of God.

2. For I determined not to know any thing among you, save Jesus Christ, and him crucified.

3. And I was with you in weakness, and in fear, and in much trembling.

4. And my speech and my preaching was not with enticing words of man's wisdom, but in demonstration of the Spirit and of power.

5. That your faith should not stand in the wisdom of men, but in the power of God.

6. Howbeit we speak wisdom among them that are perfect: yet not the wisdom of this world, that come to naught:

7. But we speak the wisdom of God in a mystery, even the hidden wisdom, which God ordained before the world unto our glory:

8. Which none of the princes of this world know: for had they known it, they would not have crucified the Lord of glory.

9. But as it is written, Eye hath not seen, nor ear heard, neither have entered into the heart of man, the things which God hath prepared for them that love him.

10. But God hath revealed them unto us by his Spirit: for the Spirit searcheth all things, yea, the deep things of God.

11. For what man knoweth the things of a man, save the spirit of man which is in him? Even so the things of God knoweth no man, but the Spirit of god.

12. Now we have received, not the spirit of the world, but the spirit which is of God; that we might know the things that are freely given to us of God.

13. Which things also we speak, not in the words which man's wisdom teacheth, but which the Holy Ghost teacheth; comparing spiritual things with spiritual.

14. But the natural man receiveth not the things of the Spirit of god; for they are foolishness unto him: neither can he know them, because they are spiritually discerned.

15. But he that is spiritual judgeth all things, yet he himself is judged of no man.

16. For who hath know the mind of the Lord, that he may instruct him? But we have the mind of Christ. (See 1 Corinthians 2: 11-16)

Richard Linford

The Jesus Christ Papers
Volume 1
The Many Witnesses that "He lives!"

Pages

1. (5)   Mary Magdalene
2. (8)   Mary Magdalene and The Other Mary and Other Women
3. (10)   Two disciples on the road to Emmaus
4. (13)   Peter
5. (14)   Ten apostles at Jerusalem
6. (15)   Eleven apostles at Jerusalem
7. (18)   Eleven disciples at the Sea of Galilee
8. (21)   Eleven disciples on a mountain in Galilee
9. (22)   More than 500 brethren at once
10. (23)   James
11. (24)   Eleven apostles at Christ's Ascension
12. (26)   Stephen
13. (34)   Paul on the road to Damascus
14. (35)   Ananias
15. (37)   Paul in jail
16. (44)   John the Beloved
17. (47)   The Four Witnesses: Matthew, Mark, Luke, John
    17.1 (47)   Matthew
    17.2 (50)   Mark
    17.3 (52)   Luke
    17.4 (54)   John
18. (57)   Book of Mormon Nephite twelve and people of Bountiful
19. (59)   Mormon
20. (59)   Moroni
21. (61)   Joseph Smith is visited by The Father and The Son
22. (65)   Joseph Smith and Oliver Cowdery are visited by The Savior
23. (65)   Joseph Smith and Sidney Rigdon see The Father and The Son
24. (68)   Modern Witnesses that Jesus Christ Lives!
    24.1 (68)   Apostle Melvin J. Ballard and President Lorenzo Snow
    24.3 (69-71) "The Living Christ" and Modern Apostles and Prophets
25. (72)   Footnote A: Ancient Secular Evidences That Jesus Christ Lived
    25.1 (72)   Josephus, Jewish Historian
    25.2 (73)   Lucien, Playwright
    25.3 (74)   Mara Bar-Serapion Letter
    25.4 (75)   Pliny the Younger, Governor of Bithynia
    25.5 (76)   Suetonius, Roman Historian
    25.6 (77)   Tacitus, Roman Historian
25. (78)   Writer's Comment
27. (79)   Writer's Background
28. (79-83) Other writings

Mary Magdalene.

Jesus first appeared to Mary. Supposing him to be a gardener, she tearfully said, "Sir, if thou have borne him hence, tell me where thou hast laid him .... Jesus saith unto her, Mary. She turned herself, and saith unto him, Rabboni; which is to say, Master." (John 20:1-18; Mark 16:9-11.)

THE GOSPEL OF JOHN CHAPTER 20

1 THE first day of the week cometh Mary Magdalene early, when it was yet dark, unto the sepulchre, and seeth the stone taken away from the sepulchre.

2 Then she runneth, and cometh to Simon Peter, and to the other disciple, whom Jesus loved, and saith unto them, They have taken away the Lord out of the sepulchre, and we know not where they have laid him.

3 Peter therefore went forth, and that other disciple, and came to the sepulchre.

4 So they ran both together: and the other disciple did outrun Peter, and came first to the sepulchre.

5 And he stooping down, and looking in, saw the linen clothes lying; yet went he not in.

6 Then cometh Simon Peter following him, and went into the sepulchre, and seeth the linen clothes lie,

7 And the napkin, that was about his head, not lying with the linen clothes, but wrapped together in a place by itself.

8 Then went in also that other disciple, which came first to the sepulchre, and he saw, and believed.

9 For as yet they knew not the scripture, that he must rise again from the dead.

10 Then the disciples went away again unto their own home.

11 But Mary stood without at the sepulchre weeping: and as she wept, she stooped down, *and looked* into the sepulchre,

12 And seeth two angels in white sitting, the one at the head, and the other at the feet, where the body of Jesus had lain.

13 And they say unto her, Woman, why weepest thou? She saith unto them, Because they have taken away my Lord, and I know not where they have laid him.

14 And when she had thus said, she turned herself back, and saw Jesus standing, and knew not that it was Jesus.

15 Jesus saith unto her, Woman, why weepest thou? whom seekest thou? She, supposing him to be the gardener, saith unto him, Sir, if thou have borne him hence, tell me where thou hast laid him, and I will take him away.

16 Jesus saith unto her, Mary. She turned herself, and saith unto him, Rabboni; which is to say, Master.

17 Jesus saith unto her, Touch me not; for I am not yet ascended to my Father: but go to my brethren, and say unto them, I ascend unto my Father, and your Father; and to my God, and your God.

18 Mary Magdalene came and told the disciples that she had seen the Lord, and that he had spoken these things unto her.

THE GOSPEL OF MARK CHAPTER 16

9 Now when Jesus was risen early the first day of the week, he appeared first to Mary Magdalene, out of whom he had cast seven devils.

10 And she went and told them that had been with him, as they mourned and wept.

11 And they, when they had heard that he was alive, and had been seen of her, believed not.

Mary of Magdala, probably the place of that name on the western shore of the Sea of Galilee.

Out of her went seven devils. (Luke 8: 2)

She was near the cross. (Matt. 27: 56; Mark 15: 40; John 19: 25)

She was at the burial. (Matt. 27: 61; Mark 15: 47)

She was at the tomb in the morning. (Matt. 28: 1; Mark 16: 1; Luke 24: 10; John 20: 1, 11

Jesus appeared to her. (Mark 16: 9; John 20: 14-18)

Mary Magdalene and the Other Mary and Other Women

As Mary Magdalene and Mary mother of Jesus left the sepulcher to tell the disciples the words of the two angels, 'Jesus met them, saying, All hail. And they came and held him by the feet, and worshipped him." (Matthew 28.1-10; Luke 24:1-11.)

THE GOSPEL OF MATTHEW CHAPTER 28

1 In the end of the sabbath, as it began to dawn toward the first day of the week, came Mary Magdalene and the other Mary to see the sepulchre.

2 And, behold, there was a great earthquake: for the angel of the Lord descended from heaven, and came and rolled back the stone from the door, and sat upon it.

3 His countenance was like lightning, and his raiment white as snow:

4 And for fear of him the keepers did shake, and became as dead men.

5 And the angel answered and said unto the women, Fear not ye: for I know that ye seek Jesus, which was crucified.

6 He is not here: for he is risen, as he said. Come, see the place where the Lord lay.

7 And go quickly, and tell his disciples that he is risen from the dead; and, behold, he goeth before you into Galilee; there shall ye see him: lo, I have told you.

8 And they departed quickly from the sepulchre with fear and great joy; and did run to bring his disciples word.

9 And as they went to tell his disciples, behold, Jesus met them, saying, All hail. And they came and held him by the feet, and worshipped him.

10 Then said Jesus unto them, Be not afraid: go tell my brethren that they go into Galilee, and there shall they see me.

THE GOSPEL OF LUKE CHAPTER 24

1 Now upon the first day of the week, very early in the morning, they came unto the sepulchre, bringing the spices which they had prepared, and certain others with them.

2 And they found the stone rolled away from the sepulchre.

3 And they entered in, and found not the body of the Lord Jesus.

4 And it came to pass, as they were much perplexed thereabout, behold, two men stood by them in shining garments:

5 And as they were afraid, and bowed down their faces to the earth, they said unto them, Why seek ye the living among the dead?

6 He is not here, but is risen: remember how he spake unto you when he was yet in Galilee,

7 Saying, The Son of man must be delivered into the hands of sinful men, and be crucified, and the third day rise again.

8 And they remembered his words,

9 And returned from the sepulchre, and told all these things unto the eleven, and to all the rest.

10 It was Mary Magdalene, and Joanna, and Mary the mother of James, and other women that were with them, which told these things unto the apostles.

11 And their words seemed to them as idle tales, and they believed them not.

Two disciples on the road to Emmaus

On the same day, as Cleopas and a companion walked toward Emmaus, Jesus "drew near, and went with them." Later, at the very moment when "he took bread, and blessed it, and brake, and gave to them," their eyes were opened, and they knew him. Then he vanished. (Luke 24:13-35.)

THE GOSPEL OF LUKE CHAPTER 24

13 And, behold, two of them went that same day to a village called Emmaus, which was from Jerusalem about threescore furlongs.

14 And they talked together of all these things which had happened.

15 And it came to pass, that, while they communed together and reasoned, Jesus himself drew near, and went with them.

16 But their eyes were holden that they should not know him.

17 And he said unto them, What manner of communications *are* these that ye have one to another, as ye walk, and are sad?

18 And the one of them, whose name was Cleopas, answering said unto him, Art thou only a stranger in Jerusalem, and hast not known the things which are come to pass there in these days?

19 And he said unto them, What things? And they said unto him, Concerning Jesus of Nazareth, which was a prophet mighty in deed and word before God and all the people:

20 And how the chief priests and our rulers delivered him to be condemned to death, and have crucified him.

21 But we trusted that it had been he which should have redeemed Israel: and beside all this, to day is the third day since these things were done.

22 Yea, and certain women also of our company made us astonished, which were early at the sepulchre;

23 And when they found not his body, they came, saying, that they had also seen a vision of angels, which said that he was alive.

24 And certain of them which were with us went to the sepulchre, and found *it* even so as the women had said: but him they saw not.

25 Then he said unto them, O fools, and slow of heart to believe all that the prophets have spoken:

26 Ought not Christ to have suffered these things, and to enter into his glory?

27 And beginning at Moses and all the prophets, he expounded unto them in all the scriptures the things concerning himself.

28 And they drew nigh unto the village, whither they went: and he made as though he would have gone further.

29 But they constrained him, saying, Abide with us: for it is toward evening, and the day is far spent. And he went in to tarry with them.

30 And it came to pass, as he sat at meat with them, he took bread, and blessed *it,* and brake, and gave to them.

31 And their eyes were opened, and they knew him; and he vanished out of their sight.

32 And they said one to another, Did not our heart burn within us, while he talked with us by the way, and while he opened to us the scriptures?

33 And they rose up the same hour, and returned to Jerusalem, and found the eleven gathered together, and them that were with them,

34 Saying, The Lord is risen indeed, and hath appeared to Simon.

35 And they told what things were done in the way, and how he was known of them in breaking of bread.

Peter

When Cleopas and his companion returned to Jerusalem, they found the 11 apostles together. The apostles told Cleopas and his friend that Jesus had risen, and "appeared to Simon." (Luke 24:33-34; 1 Corinthians 15:1-5.)

THE GOSPEL OF LUKE CHAPTER 24

33 And they rose up the same hour, and returned to Jerusalem, and found the eleven gathered together, and them that were with them,

34 Saying, The Lord is risen indeed, and hath appeared to Simon.

THE FIRST EPISTLE OF PAUL TO THE CORINTHIANS CHAPTER 15

1 MOREOVER, brethren, I declare unto you the gospel which I preached unto you, which also ye have received, and wherein ye stand;

2 By which also ye are saved, if ye keep in memory what I preached unto you, unless ye have believed in vain.

3 For I delivered unto you first of all that which I also received, how that Christ died for our sins according to the scriptures;

4 And that he was buried, and that he rose again the third day according to the scriptures:

5 And that he was seen of Cephas, then of the twelve:

Ten apostles at Jerusalem

Later that evening, 10 apostles and some disciples were gathered behind closed doors when Jesus suddenly stood in their midst and said, "Peace be unto you." Then "he shewed unto them his hands and his side. Then were the disciples glad, when they saw the Lord." (John 20:19-24.)

THE GOSPEL ACCORDING JOHN CHAPTER 20

19 Then the same day at evening, being the first *day* of the week, when the doors were shut where the disciples were assembled for fear of the Jews, came Jesus and stood in the midst, and saith unto them, Peace be unto you.

20 And when he had so said, he shewed unto them his hands and his side. Then were the disciples glad, when they saw the Lord.

21 Then said Jesus to them again, Peace be unto you: as my Father hath sent me, even so send I you.

22 And when he had said this, he breathed on them, and saith unto them, Receive ye the Holy Ghost:

23 Whose soever sins ye remit, they are remitted unto them; and whose soever sins ye retain, they are retained.

24 But Thomas, one of the twelve, called Didymus, was not with them when Jesus came.

Eleven apostles at Jerusalem

Eight days later Jesus appeared to the apostles, while Thomas, absent at the earlier appearance, was with them. "Then saith he to Thomas, Reach hither thy finger, and behold my hands; and reach hither thy hand, and thrust it into my side: and be not faithless, but believing. And Thomas answered and said unto him, My Lord and my God." (John 20:19-29; Luke 24: 33-49.)

THE GOSPEL OF JOHN CHAPTER 20

19 Then the same day at evening, being the first *day* of the week, when the doors were shut where the disciples were assembled for fear of the Jews, came Jesus and stood in the midst, and saith unto them, Peace *be* unto you.

20 And when he had so said, he shewed unto them his hands and his side. Then were the disciples glad, when they saw the Lord.

21 Then said Jesus to them again, Peace be unto you: as my Father hath sent me, even so send I you.

22 And when he had said this, he breathed on them, and saith unto them, Receive ye the Holy Ghost:

23 Whose soever sins ye remit, they are remitted unto them; and whose soever sins ye retain, they are retained.

24 But Thomas, one of the twelve, called Didymus, was not with them when Jesus came.

25 The other disciples therefore said unto him, We have seen the Lord. But he said unto them, Except I shall see in his hands the print of the nails, and put my finger into the print of the nails, and thrust my hand into his side, I will not believe.

26 And after eight days again his disciples were within, and Thomas with them: *then* came Jesus, the doors being shut, and stood in the midst, and said, Peace be unto you.

27 Then saith he to Thomas, Reach hither thy finger, and behold my hands; and reach hither thy hand, and thrust it into my side: and be not faithless, but believing.

28 And Thomas answered and said unto him, My Lord and my God.

29 Jesus saith unto him, Thomas, because thou hast seen me, thou hast believed: blessed are they that have not seen, and yet have believed.

THE GOSPEL OF LUKE CHAPTER 24

33 And they rose up the same hour, and returned to Jerusalem, and found the **eleven** gathered together, and them that were with them,

34 Saying, The Lord is risen indeed, and hath appeared to Simon.

35 And they told what things were done in the way, and how he was known of them in breaking of bread.

36 And as they thus spake, Jesus himself stood in the midst of them, and saith unto them, Peace be unto you.

37 But they were terrified and affrighted, and supposed that they had seen a spirit.

38 And he said unto them, Why are ye troubled? and why do thoughts arise in your hearts?

39 Behold my hands and my feet, that it is I myself: handle me, and see; for a spirit hath not flesh and bones, as ye see me have.

40 And when he had thus spoken, he shewed them his hands and his feet.

41 And while they yet believed not for joy, and wondered, he said unto them, Have ye here any meat?

42 And they gave him a piece of a broiled fish, and of an honeycomb.

43 And he took it, and did eat before them.

44 And he said unto them, These *are* the words which I spake unto you, while I was yet with you, that all things must be fulfilled, which were written in the law of Moses, and *in* the prophets, and *in* the psalms, concerning me.

45 Then opened he their understanding, that they might understand the scriptures,

46 And said unto them, Thus it is written, and thus it behoved Christ to suffer, and to rise from the dead the third day:

47 And that repentance and remission of sins should be preached in his name among all nations, beginning at Jerusalem.

48 And ye are witnesses of these things.

49 And, behold, I send the promise of my Father upon you: but tarry ye in the city of Jerusalem, until ye be endued with power from on high.

Eleven disciples at the Sea of Galilee

While Peter and other disciples were fishing, Jesus appeared on the shore. "Then Jesus saith unto them, Children, have ye any meat? They answered him, No. And he said unto them, Cast the net on the right side of the ship, and ye shall find. They cast therefore, and now they were not able to draw it for the multitude of fishes. Therefore that disciple whom Jesus loved saith unto Peter, It is the Lord." (John 21:1-24.)

THE GOSPEL OF JOHN CHAPTER 21

1 AFTER these things Jesus shewed himself again to the disciples at the sea of Tiberias; and on this wise shewed he himself.

2 There were together Simon Peter, and Thomas called Didymus, and Nathanael of Cana in Galilee, and the sons of Zebedee, and two other of his disciples.

3 Simon Peter saith unto them, I go a fishing. They say unto him, We also go with thee. They went forth, and entered into a ship immediately; and that night they caught nothing.

4 But when the morning was now come, Jesus stood on the shore: but the disciples knew not that it was Jesus.

5 Then Jesus saith unto them, Children, have ye any meat? They answered him, No.

6 And he said unto them, Cast the net on the right side of the ship, and ye shall find. They cast therefore, and now they were not able to draw it for the multitude of fishes.

7 Therefore that disciple whom Jesus loved saith unto Peter, It is the Lord. Now when Simon Peter heard that it was the Lord, he girt his fisher's coat unto him, (for he was naked,) and did cast himself into the sea.

8 And the other disciples came in a little ship; (for they were not far from land, but as it were two hundred cubits,) dragging the net with fishes.

9 As soon then as they were come to land, they saw a fire of coals there, and fish laid thereon, and bread.

10 Jesus saith unto them, Bring of the fish which ye have now caught.

11 Simon Peter went up, and drew the net to land full of great fishes, an hundred and fifty and three: and for all there were so many, yet was not the net broken.

12 Jesus saith unto them, Come and dine. And none of the disciples durst ask him, Who art thou? knowing that it was the Lord.

13 Jesus then cometh, and taketh bread, and giveth them, and fish likewise.

14 This is now the third time that Jesus shewed himself to his disciples, after that he was risen from the dead.

15 So when they had dined, Jesus saith to Simon Peter, Simon, son of Jonas, lovest thou me more than these? He saith unto him, Yea, Lord; thou knowest that I love thee. He saith unto him, Feed my lambs.

16 He saith to him again the second time, Simon, son of Jonas, lovest thou me? He saith unto him, Yea, Lord; thou knowest that I love thee. He saith unto him, Feed my sheep.

17 He saith unto him the third time, Simon, *son* of Jonas, lovest thou me? Peter was grieved because he said unto him the third time, Lovest thou me? And he said unto him, Lord, thou knowest all things; thou knowest that I love thee. Jesus saith unto him, Feed my sheep.

18 Verily, verily, I say unto thee, When thou wast young, thou girdedst thyself, and walkedst whither thou wouldest: but when thou shalt be old, thou shalt stretch forth thy hands, and another shall gird thee, and carry thee whither thou wouldest not.

19 This spake he, signifying by what death he should glorify God. And when he had spoken this, he saith unto him, Follow me.

20 Then Peter, turning about, seeth the disciple whom Jesus loved following; which also leaned on his breast at supper, and said, Lord, which is he that betrayeth thee?

21 Peter seeing him saith to Jesus, Lord, and what shall this man do?

22 Jesus saith unto him, If I will that he tarry till I come, what is that to thee? follow thou me.

23 Then went this saying abroad among the brethren, that that disciple should not die: yet Jesus said not unto him, He shall not die; but, If I will that he tarry till I come, what is that to thee?

24 This is the disciple which testifieth of these things, and wrote these things: and we know that his testimony is true.

Eleven disciples on a mountain in Galilee

"And Jesus came and spake unto them, saying, All power is given unto me in heaven and in earth." (Matthew 28:16-18.)

THE GOSPEL OF MATTHEW CHAPTER 28

16 Then the eleven disciples went away into Galilee, into a mountain where Jesus had appointed them.

17 And when they saw him, they worshipped him: but some doubted.

18 And Jesus came and spake unto them, saying, All power is given unto me in heaven and in earth.

19 Go ye therefore, and teach all nations, baptizing them in the name of the Father, and of the Son, and of the Holy Ghost:

20 Teaching them to observe all things whatsoever I have commanded you: and, lo, I am with you alway, even unto the end of the world. Amen.

More than 500 brethren at once

"After that, he was seen of above five hundred brethren at once ...." (1 Corinthians 15:6.)

THE FIRST EPISTLE OF PAUL TO THE CORINTHIANS CHAPTER 15

6 After that, he was seen of above five hundred brethren at once; of whom the greater part remain unto this present, but some are fallen asleep.

James

"After that, he was seen of James ...." (1 Corinthians 15:7.)

THE FIRST EPISTLE OF PAUL TO THE CORINTHIANS CHAPTER 15

7 After that, he was seen of James; then of all the apostles.

Eleven apostles at Christ's Ascension

"And he led them out as far as to Bethany, and he lifted up his hands, and blessed them. And it came to pass, while he blessed them, he was parted from them, and carried up into heaven." (Luke 24:50-51; Mark 16:19.)

THE GOSPEL ACCORDING TO LUKE CHAPTER 24

50 And he led them out as far as to Bethany, and he lifted up his hands, and blessed them.

51 And it came to pass, while he blessed them, he was parted from them, and carried up into heaven.

52 And they worshipped him, and returned to Jerusalem with great joy:

53 And were continually in the temple, praising and blessing God. Amen.

THE GOSPEL ACCORDING TO MARK CHAPTER 16

He ascends into heaven.

14 Afterward he appeared unto the eleven as they sat at meat, and upbraided them with their unbelief and hardness of heart, because they believed not them which had seen him after he was risen.

15 And he said unto them, Go ye into all the world, and preach the gospel to every creature.

16 He that believeth and is baptized shall be saved; but he that believeth not shall be damned.

17 And these signs shall follow them that believe; In my name shall they cast out devils; they shall speak with new tongues;

18 They shall take up serpents; and if they drink any deadly thing, it shall not hurt them: they shall lay hands on the sick, and they shall recover.

19 So then after the Lord had spoken unto them, he was received up into heaven, and sat on the right hand of God.

20 And they went forth, and preached every where, the Lord working with *them,* and confirming the word with signs following. Amen.

Stephen

After making a speech to the Sanhedrin, Stephen, "looked up steadfastly into heaven, and saw the glory of God, and Jesus standing on the right hand of God. And said, Behold, I see the heavens opened, and the Son of man standing on the right hand of God." (Acts 6:9-7:56.)

THE ACTS OF THE APOSTLES CHAPTER 6

1 AND in those days, when the number of the disciples was multiplied, there arose a murmuring of the Grecians against the Hebrews, because their widows were neglected in the daily ministrations.

2 Then the twelve called the multitude of the disciples unto them, and said, It is not reason that we should leave the word of God, and serve tables.

3 Wherefore, brethren, look ye out among you seven men of honest report, full of the Holy Ghost and wisdom, whom we may appoint over this business.

4 But we will give ourselves continually to prayer, and to the ministry of the word.

5 And the saying pleased the whole multitude: and they chose Stephen, a man full of faith and of the Holy Ghost, and Philip, and Prochorus, and Nicanor, and Timon, and Parmenas, and Nicolas a proselyte of Antioch:

6 Whom they set before the apostles: and when they had prayed, they laid their hands on them.

7 And the word of God increased; and the number of the disciples multiplied in Jerusalem greatly; and a great company of the priests were obedient to the faith.

8 And Stephen, full of faith and power, did great wonders and miracles among the people.

9 Then there arose certain of the synagogue, which is called the synagogue of the Libertines, and Cyrenians, and Alexandrians, and of them of Cilicia and of Asia, disputing with Stephen.

10 And they were not able to resist the wisdom and the spirit by which he spake.

11 Then they suborned men, which said, We have heard him speak blasphemous words against Moses, and against God.

12 And they stirred up the people, and the elders, and the scribes, and came upon him, and caught him, and brought him to the council,

13 And set up false witnesses, which said, This man ceaseth not to speak blasphemous words against this holy place, and the law:

14 For we have heard him say, that this Jesus of Nazareth shall destroy this place, and shall change the customs which Moses delivered us.

15 And all that sat in the council, looking stedfastly on him, saw his face as it had been the face of an angel.

THE ACTS OF THE APOSTLES CHAPTER 7

Stephen recounts the history of Israel and names Moses as a prototype of Christ—He testifies of the apostasy in Israel—He sees Jesus on the right hand of God—Stephen's testimony is rejected and he is stoned to death.

1 THEN said the high priest, Are these things so?

2 And he said, Men, brethren, and fathers, hearken; The God of glory appeared unto our father Abraham, when he was in Mesopotamia, before he dwelt in Charran,

3 And said unto him, Get thee out of thy country, and from thy kindred, and come into the land which I shall shew thee.

4 Then came he out of the land of the Chaldeans, and dwelt in Charran: and from thence, when his father was dead, he removed him into this land, wherein ye now dwell.

5 And he gave him none inheritance in it, no, not *so much as* to set his foot on: yet he promised that he would give it to him for a possession, and to his seed after him, when *as yet* he had no child.

6 And God spake on this wise, That his seed should sojuourn in a strange land; and that they should bring them into bondage, and entreat them evil four hundred years.

7 And the nation to whom they shall be in bondage will I judge, said God: and after that shall they come forth, and serve me in this place.

8 And he gave him the covenant of circumcision: and so *Abraham* begat Isaac, and circumcised him the eighth day; and Isaac begat Jacob; and Jacob begat the twelve patriarchs.

9 And the patriarchs, moved with envy, sold Joseph into Egypt: but God was with him,

10 And delivered him out of all his afflictions, and gave him favour and wisdom in the sight of Pharaoh king of Egypt; and he made him governor over Egypt and all his house.

11 Now there came a dearth over all the land of Egypt and Chanaan, and great affliction: and our fathers found no sustenance.

12 But when Jacob heard that there was corn in Egypt, he sent out our fathers first.

13 And at the second time Joseph was made known to his brethren; and Joseph's kindred was made known unto Pharaoh.

14 Then sent Joseph, and called his father Jacob to him, and all his kindred, threescore and fifteen souls.

15 So Jacob went down into Egypt, and died, he, and our fathers,

16 And were carried over into Sychem, and laid in the sepulchre that Abraham bought for a sum of money of the sons of Emmor the father of Sychem.

17 But when the time of the promise drew nigh, which God had sworn to Abraham, the people grew and multiplied in Egypt,

18 Till another king arose, which knew not Joseph.

19 The same dealt subtilly with our kindred, and evil entreated our fathers, so that they cast out their young children, to the end they might not live.

20 In which time Moses was born, and was exceeding fair, and nourished up in his father's house three months:

21 And when he was cast out, Pharaoh's daughter took him up, and nourished him for her own son.

22 And Moses was learned in all the wisdom of the Egyptians, and was mighty in words and in deeds.

23 And when he was full forty years old, it came into his heart to visit his brethren the children of Israel.

24 And seeing one of them suffer wrong, he defended him, and avenged him that was oppressed, and smote the Egyptian:

25 For he supposed his brethren would have understood how that God by his hand would deliver them: but they understood not.

26 And the next day he shewed himself unto them as they strove, and would have set them at one again, saying, Sirs, ye are brethren; why do ye wrong one to another?

27 But he that did his neighbour wrong thrust him away, saying, Who made thee a ruler and a judge over us?

28 Wilt thou kill me, as thou diddest the Egyptian yesterday?

29 Then fled Moses at this saying, and was a stranger in the land of Madian, where he begat two sons.

30 And when forty years were expired, there appeared to him in the wilderness of mount Sina an angel of the Lord in a flame of fire in a bush.

31 When Moses saw *it,* he wondered at the sight: and as he drew near to behold it, the voice of the Lord came unto him,

32 Saying, I am the God of thy fathers, the God of Abraham, and the God of Isaac, and the God of Jacob. Then Moses trembled, and durst not behold.

33 Then said the Lord to him, Put off thy shoes from thy feet: for the place where thou standest is holy ground.

34 I have seen, I have seen the affliction of my people which is in Egypt, and I have heard their groaning, and am come down to deliver them. And now come, I will send thee into Egypt.

35 This Moses whom they refused, saying, Who made thee a ruler and a judge? the same did God send to be a ruler and a deliverer by the hand of the angel which appeared to him in the bush.

58 And cast him out of the city, and stoned him: and the witnesses laid down their clothes at a young man's feet, whose name was Saul.

59 And they stoned Stephen, calling upon God, and saying, Lord Jesus, receive my spirit.

60 And he kneeled down, and cried with a loud voice, Lord, lay not this sin to their charge. And when he had said this, he fell asleep.

Paul on the road to Damascus

"And as he [Paul] journeyed, he came near Damascus: and suddenly there shined round about him a light from heaven .... And he said, Who art thou, Lord? And the Lord said, I am Jesus ..." (Acts 9:3-5.)

THE ACTS OF THE APOSTLES CHAPTER 9

1 AND Saul, yet breathing out threatenings and slaughter against the disciples of the Lord, went unto the high priest,

2 And desired of him letters to Damascus to the synagogues, that if he found any of this way, whether they were men or women, he might bring them bound unto Jerusalem.

3 And as he journeyed, he came near Damascus: and suddenly there shined round about him a light from heaven:

4 And he fell to the earth, and heard a voice saying unto him, Saul, Saul, why persecutest thou me?

5 And he said, Who art thou, Lord? And the Lord said, I am Jesus whom thou persecutest: *it is* hard for thee to kick against the pricks.

6 And he trembling and astonished said, Lord, what wilt thou have me to do? And the Lord *said* unto him, Arise, and go into the city, and it shall be told thee what thou must do.

7 And the men which journeyed with him stood speechless, hearing a voice, but seeing no man.

8 And Saul arose from the earth; and when his eyes were opened, he saw no man: but they led him by the hand, and brought him into Damascus.

9 And he was three days without sight, and neither did eat nor drink.

Ananias

"And there was a certain disciple at Damascus, named Ananias, and to him said the Lord in a vision, Ananias. And he said, Behold, I am here, Lord." (Acts 9:10.)

THE ACTS OF THE APOSTLES CHAPTER 9

10 And there was a certain disciple at Damascus, named Ananias; and to him said the Lord in a vision, Ananias. And he said, Behold, I am here, Lord.

11 And the Lord said unto him, Arise, and go into the street which is called Straight, and enquire in the house of Judas for one called Saul, of Tarsus: for, behold, he prayeth,

12 And hath seen in a vision a man named Ananias coming in, and putting his hand on him, that he might receive his sight.

13 Then Ananias answered, Lord, I have heard by many of this man, how much evil he hath done to thy saints at Jerusalem:

14 And here he hath authority from the chief priests to bind all that call on thy name.

15 But the Lord said unto him, Go thy way: for he is a chosen vessel unto me, to bear my name before the Gentiles, and kings, and the children of Israel:

16 For I will shew him how great things he must suffer for my name's sake.

17 And Ananias went his way, and entered into the house; and putting his hands on him said, Brother Saul, the Lord, even Jesus, that appeared unto thee in the way as thou camest, hath sent me, that thou mightest receive thy sight, and be filled with the Holy Ghost.

18 And immediately there fell from his eyes as it had been scales: and he received sight forthwith, and arose, and was baptized.

19 And when he had received meat, he was strengthened. Then was Saul certain days with the disciples which were at Damascus.

20 And straightway he preached Christ in the synagogues, that he is the Son of God.

21 But all that heard him were amazed, and said; Is not this he that destroyed them which called on this name in Jerusalem, and came hither for that intent, that he might bring them bound unto the chief priests?

22 But Saul increased the more in strength, and confounded the Jews which dwelt at Damascus, proving that this is very Christ.

Paul in jail

Paul was put in jail in Caesarea. "And the night following the Lord stood by him, and said, Be of good cheer, Paul: for thou hast testified of me in Jerusalem, so must thou bear witness also at Rome." (Acts 22-23.)

THE ACTS OF THE APOSTLES CHAPTER 22

1 MEN, brethren, and fathers, hear ye my defence which I make now unto you.

2 (And when they heard that he spake in the Hebrew tongue to them, they kept the more silence: and he saith,)

3 I am verily a man which am a Jew, born in Tarsus, *a city* in Cilicia, yet brought up in this city at the feet of Gamaliel, and taught according to the perfect manner of the law of the fathers, and was zealous toward God, as ye all are this day.

4 And I persecuted this way unto the death, binding and delivering into prisons both men and women.

5 As also the high priest doth bear me witness, and all the estate of the elders: from whom also I received letters unto the brethren, and went to Damascus, to bring them which were there bound unto Jerusalem, for to be punished.

6 And it came to pass, that, as I made my journey, and was come nigh unto Damascus about noon, suddenly there shone from heaven a great light round about me.

7 And I fell unto the ground, and heard a voice saying unto me, Saul, Saul, why persecutest thou me?

8 And I answered, Who art thou, Lord? And he said unto me, I am Jesus of Nazareth, whom thou persecutest.

9 And they that were with me saw indeed the light, and were afraid; but they heard not the voice of him that spake to me.

10 And I said, What shall I do, Lord? And the Lord said unto me, Arise, and go into Damascus; and there it shall be told thee of all things which are appointed for thee to do.

11 And when I could not see for the glory of that light, being led by the hand of them that were with me, I came into Damascus.

12 And one Ananias, a devout man according to the law, having a good report of all the Jews which dwelt there,

13 Came unto me, and stood, and said unto me, Brother Saul, receive thy sight. And the same hour I looked up upon him.

14 And he said, The God of our fathers hath chosen thee, that thou shouldest know his will, and see that Just One, and shouldest hear the voice of his mouth.

15 For thou shalt be his witness unto all men of what thou hast seen and heard.

16 And now why tarriest thou? arise, and be baptized, and wash away thy sins, calling on the name of the Lord.

17 And it came to pass, that, when I was come again to Jerusalem, even while I prayed in the temple, I was in a trance;

18 And saw him saying unto me, Make haste, and get thee quickly out of Jerusalem: for they will not receive thy testimony concerning me.

19 And I said, Lord, they know that I imprisoned and beat in every synagogue them that believed on thee:

20 And when the blood of thy martyr Stephen was shed, I also was standing by, and consenting unto his death, and kept the raiment of them that slew him.

21 And he said unto me, Depart: for I will send thee far hence unto the Gentiles.

22 And they gave him audience unto this word, and then lifted up their voices, and said, Away with such a fellow from the earth: for it is not fit that he should live.

23 And as they cried out, and cast off their clothes, and threw dust into the air,

24 The chief captain commanded him to be brought into the castle, and bade that he should be examined by scourging; that he might know wherefore they cried so against him.

25 And as they bound him with thongs, Paul said unto the centurion that stood by, Is it lawful for you to scourge a man that is a Roman, and uncondemned?

26 When the centurion heard *that,* he went and told the chief captain, saying, Take heed what thou doest: for this man is a Roman.

27 Then the chief captain came, and said unto him, Tell me, art thou a Roman? He said, Yea.

28 And the chief captain answered, With a great sum obtained I this freedom. And Paul said, But I was free born.

29 Then straightway they departed from him which should have examined him: and the chief captain also was afraid, after he knew that he was a Roman, and because he had bound him.

30 On the morrow, because he would have known the certainty wherefore he was accused of the Jews, he loosed him from *his* bands, and commanded the chief priests and all their council to appear, and brought Paul down, and set him before them.

THE ACTS OF THE APOSTLES CHAPTER 23

Paul smitten at Ananias' order. The Lord again appears to Paul. Forty Jews plot his death. He is delivered over to Felix.

1 AND Paul, earnestly beholding the council, said, Men and brethren, I have lived in all good conscience before God until this day.

2 And the high priest Ananias commanded them that stood by him to smite him on the mouth.

3 Then said Paul unto him, God shall smite thee, thou whited wall: for sittest thou to judge me after the law, and commandest me to be smitten contrary to the law?

4 And they that stood by said, Rivilest thou God's high priest?

5 Then said Paul, I wist not, brethren, that he was the high priest: for it is written, Thou shalt not speak evil of the ruler of thy people.

6 But when Paul perceived that the one part were Sadducees, and the other Pharisees, he cried out in the council, Men and brethren, I am a Pharisee, the son of a Pharisee: of the hope and resurrection of the dead I am called in question.

7 And when he had so said, there arose a dissension between the Pharisees and the Sadducees: and the multitude was divided.

8 For the Sadducees say that there is no resurrection, neither angel, nor spirit: but the Pharisees confess both.

9 And there arose a great cry: and the scribes that were of the Pharisees' part arose, and strove, saying, We find no evil in this man: but if a spirit or an angel hath spoken to him, let us not fight against God.

10 And when there arose a great dissension, the chief captain, fearing lest Paul should have been pulled in pieces of them, commanded the soldiers to go down, and to take him by force from among them, and to bring him into the castle.

11 And the night following the Lord stood by him, and said, Be of good cheer, Paul: for as thou hast testified of me in Jerusalem, so must thou bear witness also at Rome.

12 And when it was day, certain of the Jews banded together, and bound themselves under a curse, saying that they would neither eat nor drink till they had killed Paul.

13 And they were more than forty which had made this conspiracy.

14 And they came to the chief priests and elders, and said, We have bound ourselves under a great curse, that we will eat nothing until we have slain Paul.

15 Now therefore ye with the council signify to the chief captain that he bring him down unto you to morrow, as though ye would enquire something more perfectly concerning him: and we, or ever he come near, are ready to kill him.

16 And when Paul's sister's son heard of their lying in wait, he went and entered into the castle, and told Paul.

17 Then Paul called one of the centurions unto him, and said, Bring this young man unto the chief captain: for he hath a certain thing to tell him.

18 So he took him, and brought him to the chief captain, and said, Paul the prisoner called me unto him, and prayed me to bring this young man unto thee, who hath something to say unto thee.

19 Then the chief captain took him by the hand, and went with him aside privately, and asked him, What is that thou hast to tell me?

20 And he said, The Jews have agreed to desire thee that thou wouldest bring down Paul to morrow into the council, as though they would enquire somewhat of him more perfectly.

21 But do not thou yield unto them: for there lie in wait for him of them more than forty men, which have bound themselves with an oath, that they will neither eat nor drink till they have killed him: and now are they ready, looking for a promise from thee.

22 So the chief captain then let the young man depart, and charged him, See thou tell no man that thou hast shewed these things to me.

23 And he called unto him two centurions, saying, Make ready two hundred soldiers to go to Caesarea, and horsemen threescore and ten, and spearmen two hundred, at the third hour of the night;

24 And provide them beasts, that they may set Paul on, and bring him safe unto Felix the governor.

25 And he wrote a letter after this manner:

26 Claudius Lysias unto the most excellent governor Felix sendeth greeting.

27 This man was taken of the Jews, and should have been killed of them: then came I with an army, and rescued him, having understood that he was a Roman.

28 And when I would have known the cause wherefore they accused him, I brought him forth into their council:

29 Whom I perceived to be accused of questions of their law, but to have nothing laid to his charge worthy of death or of bonds.

30 And when it was told me how that the Jews laid wait for the man, I sent straightway to thee, and gave commandment to his accusers also to say before thee what they had against him. Farewell.

31 Then the soldiers, as it was commanded them, took Paul, and brought him by night to Antipatris.

32 On the morrow they left the horsemen to go with him, and returned to the castle:

33 Who, when they came to Caesarea, and delivered the epistle to the governor, presented Paul also before him.

34 And when the governor had read the letter, he asked of what province he was. And when he understood that he was of Cilicia;

35 I will hear thee, said he, when thine accusers are also come. And he commanded him to be kept in Herod's judgment hall.

John the Beloved

John saw "one like unto the Son of man, clothed with a garment down to the foot, and girt about the paps with a golden girdle. His head and his hairs were white like wool, as white as snow; and his eyes were as a flame of fire; And his feet like unto fine brass, as if they burned in a furnace; and his voice as the sound of many waters." (Revelation 1:13-15.)

THE REVELATION OF JOHN THE BELOVED CHAPTER 1

1 THE Revelation of Jesus Christ, which God gave unto him, to shew unto his servants things which must shortly come to pass; and he sent and signified it by his angel unto his servant John:

2 Who bare record of the word of God, and of the testimony of Jesus Christ, and of all things that he saw.

3 Blessed is he that readeth, and they that hear the words of this prophecy, and keep those things which are written therein: for the time is at hand.

4 JOHN to the seven churches which are in Asia: Grace be unto you, and peace, from him which is, and which was, and which is to come; and from the seven Spirits which are before his throne;

5 And from Jesus Christ, who is the faithful witness, and the first begotten of the dead, and the prince of the kings of the earth. Unto him that loved us, and washed us from our sins in his own blood,

6 And hath made us kings and priests unto God and his Father; to him be glory and dominion for ever and ever. Amen.

7 Behold, he cometh with clouds; and every eye shall see him, and they also which pierced him: and all kindreds of the earth shall wail because of him. Even so, Amen.

8 I am Alpha and Omega, the beginning and the ending, saith the Lord, which is, and which was, and which is to come, the Almighty.

9 I John, who also am your brother, and companion in tribulation, and in the kingdom and patience of Jesus Christ, was in the isle that is called Patmos, for the word of God, and for the testimony of Jesus Christ.

10 I was in the Spirit on the Lord's day, and heard behind me a great voice, as of a trumpet,

11 Saying, I am Alpha and Omega, the first and the last: and, What thou seest, write in a book, and send it unto the seven churches which are in Asia; unto Ephesus, and unto Smyrna, and unto Pergamos, and unto Thyatira, and unto Sardis, and unto Philadelphia, and unto Laodicea.

12 And I turned to see the voice that spake with me. And being turned, I saw seven golden candlesticks;

13 And in the midst of the seven candlesticks one like unto the Son of man, clothed with a garment down to the foot, and girt about the paps with a golden girdle.

14 His head and his hairs were white like wool, as white as snow; and his eyes were as a flame of fire;

15 And his feet like unto fine brass, as if they burned in a furnace; and his voice as the sound of many waters.

16 And he had in his right hand seven stars: and out of his mouth went a sharp twoedged sword: and his countenance was as the sun shineth in his strength.

17 And when I saw him, I fell at his feet as dead. And he laid his right hand upon me, saying unto me, Fear not; I am the first and the last:

18 *I am* he that liveth, and was dead; and, behold, I am alive for evermore, Amen; and have the keys of hell and of death.

19 Write the things which thou hast seen, and the things which are, and the things which shall be hereafter;

20 The mystery of the seven stars which thou sawest in my right hand, and the seven golden candlesticks. The seven stars are the angels of the seven churches: and the seven candlesticks which thou sawest are the seven churches.

The Four Witnesses: Matthew, Mark, Luke, and John

Matthew

Matthew (Levi) the Apostle, testifies of Christ in his Gospel of Matthew. "And as Jesus passed forth from thence, he saw a man, named Matthew, sitting at the receipt of custom: and he saith unto him, Follow me. And he arose, and followed him." (Matthew 9:9, 9-13) "And after these things he went forth, and saw a publican, named Levi, sitting at the receipt of custom: and he said unto him, Follow me." (Luke 5:27, 27-32) Matthew testifies of Christ's atonement and resurrection. He sees "Christianity as the culmination of Judaism, with Jesus as the promised Messiah. In many details of Jesus' life, Matthew saw fulfillment of Old Testament prophecy … ." (Encyclopedia of Mormonism, Macmillen 1992, page 869.)

"Matthew. Gift of God. Known before his conversion as Levi, son of Alphaeus (Mark 2:14). He was a tax gatherer at Capernaum, probably in the service of Herod Antipas, in whose tetrarchy Capernaum was. Soon after his call he gave a feast to his old associates (Matthew 9:9-13; Mark 2:14-17; Luke 5:27-32) at which the Lord was present, and was in consequence blamed by the Pharisees. Matthew was probably a thorough Jew with a wide knowledge of the Old Testament scriptures, and able to see in every detail of the Lord's life the fulfillment of prophecy. His Gospel (see Gospels) was written for the use of Jewish persons in Palestine, and uses many quotations from the Old Testament. His chief object is to show that Jesus is the Messiah of whom the prophets spoke. He also emphasizes that Jesus is the King and Judge of men. His Gospel was probably written in Aramaic, but is known to us by a Greek translation. Of the apostle's later life little is known for certain. A tradition asserts that he died a martyr's death." (LDS Scriptures, Bible Dictionary, p. 729)

"Matthew testifies of Christ's birth and name (Matthew chapter 1); of the mission of the wise men, of flight into Egypt by Joseph, Mary, and Jesus, of Herod's slaying of the Bethlehem children, of the family's relocation to Nazareth (Mt.c2); of John the Baptist's preaching, of Jesus' baptism, and of the Father's acclamation that Jesus is his Beloved Son (Mt.c3); Matthew tells of our Savior's forty day fast and temptations, of the beginning of his ministry, the calling of his disciples, of healing the sick (Mt. c4); Matthew preserves for us the Sermon on the Mount with Christ's promise of salvation to all who believe in him and do the will of the Father (Mt. c5, 6,7); In Matthew we read of healing a leper, curing a servant of a centurion, casting out devils and the herd of swine (Mt.c8); of Jesus forgiving sins, healing a paralytic, calling Matthew, eating with sinners, healing a woman who touched his garments, raising Jairus' daughter to life, opening the eyes of the blind, casting out a devil, and preaching the gospel (Mt.c9); we learn of Christ's instruction to, empowerment of , and sending out the Twelve Apostles to preach, minister, and heal the sick (Mt.c10); we read of his testimony of John, of upbraiding the people of certain cities for their unbelief; we read of his role as The Son who reveals The Father, of the lightness and easiness of his burden (Mt.c11); of being Lord of the Sabbath, and of his serious conflict with the Pharisees (Mt.c12); we read the parables of the sower, wheat and the tares, grain of mustard seed, leaven, treasure hid in the field, pearl of great price, and net cast into the sea, and we appreciate in part the sadness Jesus experienced in not being honored as prophet and Messiah by his own people in Nazareth for they thought of him merely as "the carpenter's son" "whose mother is Mary and whose brethren are James, Joses, Simon, and Judas, "and his sisters, are they not all with us?"; we hear Jesus' lament "A prophet is not without honour, save in his own country, and in his own house. And he did not many mighty works there because of their unbelief." (Mt.c13); we feel pathos at the beheading of John the Baptist, amazement at his feeding the five thousand and walking on water (Mt.c14); and sadness he was called upon to suffer great contentions with scribes and Pharisees; our faith is lifted at his healing of the daughter of a Gentile woman, at his feeding the four thousand (Mt.c15); we are warned against the leaven or doctrine of the Pharisees and Sadducees; Matthew preserves for us Peter's testimony that Jesus is the Christ, the doctrine of promised priesthood keys of the kingdom, Jesus' prophecy about His death and resurrection (Mt.c16); and we see through a veil darkly the transfiguration of Peter, James, and John on the mount; we experience his healing of a lunatic; we hear the Savior foretelling his coming death, and in all of this we note his pause to pay taxes miraculously using a coin found in the mouth of a fish (Mt.c17); we learn how apostles and disciples ought to treat offending brethren; we rejoice at The Son of Man's role in saving that which was lost; in his giving all of the Twelve the keys of the kingdom, and we pay particular attention when he teaches us why we should forgive (Mt.c18); we learn of marriage and divorce, of eternal life being reserved for those who keep God's commandments, and the sobering truth that The Twelve Apostles will judge the house of Israel (Mt.c19); we appreciate in part the parable of the laborers in the vineyard, of Jesus foretelling his crucifixion and his resurrection, of his giving his life a ransom for many (Mt.c20); Matthew testifies of his triumphal entry into Jerusalem, cleansing the temple, cursing the fig tree, the parable of the two sons, and the wicked husbandmen (Mt.c21); we are taught the parable of a marriage of the king's son, the duty to pay tribute to Caesar and to God, the fact worldly marriages endure in this life only, and greatest of all his teachings, we are taught the first and great commandments to "love the Lord thy God with all thy heart, and with all thy soul, and with all thy mind" and to "love thy neighbor as thyself" for "on these two commandments hang all the law and the prophets Mt.c22); he pronounced woes on the scribes and Pharisees (Mt.c23); foretold the destruction of Jerusalem and temple and great calamities that precede his Second Coming, and we learn the parable of the fig tree (Mt.c24); and the parables of the ten virgins, the talents, and the sheep and the goats (Mt.c25); we weep at his suffering in Gethsemane, and we are appalled at his betrayal by Judas, at his being taken before Caiaphas, at Peter's "thrice" denial that he knew him (Mt.c26); we are angered at his accusation and condemnation before Pilate, the unjust release of Barabbas, at the inhumane mockery and crucifixion he suffered; and we read of His burial in the tomb of Joseph of Arimathaea (Mt.c27); we experience the joy of his resurrection; we joy in his appearances, and his ascension to the Father where he was before, and Matthew testifies that now he has all power in heaven and in earth, and recounts his straightforward directive is to his apostles to go into all the world and teach and baptize all nations. (Mt.c28). (New Testament King James Version, LDSV)

Mark

Mark in his Gospel of Mark, testifies that Jesus is the Christ.

"Mark. Also called John; son of Mary, who had a house of considerable size in Jerusalem (Acts 13:12); cousin (or nephew) of Barnabas (Col 4:10); accompanied Paul and Barnabas from Jerusalem (Acts 12:25) and on their first missionary journey, deserting them at Perga (13:5,13); accompanied Barnabas to Cyprus (15:37-39); with Paul at Rome (Col. 4:10; Philem. 1:24); with Peter at Babylon (i.e. probably at Rome) (1 Pet. 5:13); with Timothy at Ephesus (2 Tim. 4:11). His gospel (see Gospels) was possibly written under the direction of Peter. His object is to describe our Lord as the incarnate Son of God, living and acting amoung men. The Gospel contains a living picture of a living man. Energy and humility are the characteristics of his portrait. It is full of descriptive touches that help us to realize the impression made upon the bystanders. Tradition states that after Peter's death, Mark visited Egypt, founded the Church of Alexandria, and died by martyrdom." (LDS Scriptures, Bible Dictionary, page 728)

A shorter gospel, "Mark testifies of Jesus' baptism by John, how Jesus preached the gospel, how He called disciples, cast out devils, healed the sick, and cleansed a leper (Mark chapter 1); Mark tells how he forgave and forgives sins, healed a paralytic, ate with publicans and sinners, how he testified that he is Lord of the Sabbath (Mc2); Mark tells how Jesus healed on the Sabbath, chose and ordained Twelve Apostles, asked "Can Satan cast out Satan?, spoke of blasphemy against the Holy Ghost, and identified all who believe as members of his family, stating "whosoever shall do the will of God, the same is my brother, and my sister, and mother." (Mc3; c3:38); Mark gives us the parables of the sower, the candle under a bushel, the seed growing secretly, and the parable of the mustard seed; we read of how the Savior, on hearing the words from his disciples "Master, carest thou not that we perish?", stills a powerful tempest (Mc4; c438); Mark recounts how Jesus cast out a legion of devils that went into swine, of a woman healed by touching his clothes, and how He raised Jairus' daughter from the dead (mc5); of his sending forth the Twelve, of the beheading of John by Herod, of feeding the five thousand, walking on water, of healing multitudes (Mc6); of reproving the Pharisees for their false traditions and ceremonies, of casting a devil out of the daughter of a Greek woman, of opening the ears and loosening the tongue of one with a speech impediment (Mc7); of feeding the four thousand, of counseling "Beware of the leaven of the Pharisees," of healing a blind man in Bethsaida, and of Peter's testimony "Thou art the Christ" (Mc8); Mark testifies of the transfiguration, of Jesus' casting out a dumb and deaf spirit, of the master's teachings concerning death and the resurrection and who shall be greatest among you; Mark tells us of Christ's cursing those who "offend one of these little ones that believe in me" (Mc9, c9:42); Mark speaks of Jesus' teachings regarding the higher law of marriage, blessing little children, counseling the rich young man, foretelling his own death, healing blind Bartimaeus (Mc10); in Mark we learn of Christ's ride into Jerusalem on a colt midst shouts of Hosanna, of cursing a fig tree, driving the money changers from the temple, discomfiting the scribes on the matter of authority (Mc11); we learn the parable of the wicked husbandmen, of paying taxes, of celestial marriage, and Mark gives us the two great commandments; then we read the testimony of the divine Sonship of Christ, and the great story of sacrifice of the widow's mites (Mc12); Mark tells of Jesus' prophecy of great calamities and signs to precede His Second Coming, of false Christs and false prophets, of the parable of the fig tree (Mc13); of Christ's anointing with oil, of eating the Passover, instituting the sacrament, suffering in Gethsemane; and betrayal by Judas; we read of false accusations, and of Peter denying that he knows Jesus (Mc14); of Pilate decreeing Jesus' death, of mocking and cruel crucifixion between two thieves, of Christ's death and burial in the tomb of Joseph of Arimathaea (Mc15); Mark testifies that Jesus is risen, appeared to Mary Magdalene, then to others, and that the Savior sent the apostles to preach, promising that signs shall follow their faith in him; and lastly, Mark declares that Our Lord Jesus Christ ascended into heaven. (Mc16). (New Testament King James Version, LDSV)

Luke

Luke in his Gospel of Luke and Book of Acts testifies that Jesus Christ lives and is the Savior of the world.

Luke is "mentioned three times in the New Testament (Col. 4:14; 2 Tim. 4:11); Philem. 1:24). He was also the writer of the third Gospel and of the Acts. In all passages in the latter book in which the first person plural is used (e.g., Acts 16:10), we can assume that Luke was Paul's fellow-traveler. He was born of gentile parents, and practiced medicine. He may have become a believer before our Lord's ascension, but there is no evidence of this. The identification of him with one of the disciples to whom our Lord appeared on the way to Emmaus is picturesque but historically unsupported. The first information about him is when he joined Paul at Troas (Acts 16:10); his medical knowledge would make him a welcome companion. He seems to have remained at Philippi for several years, as Paul found him there on his last journey to Jerusalem (20:6), and the two were together until there arrival in Rome. We learn from 2 Tim. 4:11 that Luke was with Paul during his second Roman imprisonment, was written; it was specially intended for gentile readers. The Acts was a continuation of the Gospel, and deals mainly with the growth of the gentile churches. History tells us nothing of Luke's later years, but tradition says he died a martyr. JST Luke 1:1 attributes to Luke a high calling as a "messenger of Jesus Christ." (LDS Scriptures, Bible Dictionary pp. 726-727)

"Luke describes Gabriel's promises to Zacharias and Elisabeth that they shall have a son John; Luke testifies that Jesus is Son of the Father and of Mary's calling to serve as His mother and Luke restates Mary's great Psalm of praise; Luke tells of the birth of John and the prophesies of Zacharias about his son John (Luke chapter 1); Luke speaks of angels heralding the birth of Jesus in Bethlehem, of prophesies by Simeon and Anna, and of Jesus teaching in the temple at age twelve (Lc2); we learn of John's preaching and baptizing including the baptism of Jesus and Luke recounts the Savior's genealogy (Lc3); we read of Jesus' forty day fast and temptations of the devil, of his statement to those in the synagogue in Nazareth that He is the Son of God, of casting out a devil in Capernaum and healing Peter's mother-in-law, and of preaching and healing in Galilee (Lc4); we read of the fisherman Peter who was called to fish men, of Jesus' healing of a leper, of forgiving sins and healing a paralytic, of calling Matthew, of teaching that the sick not those who are well need the physician, and that new wine of his gospel is to be poured into new bottles (Lc5); we learn of healing on the Sabbath, choosing the Twelve Apostles, blessings to those who are obedient and cursing of those who are wicked (Lc6); we read of healing the centurion's servant, raising from the dead son of the widow of

Nain; of Jesus extolling John the Baptist as more than a prophet, of a woman anointing Christ's feet, and of his forgiveness of her sins (Lc7); we read the parable of the sower, stilling the tempest, casting out a legion of devils and the herd of swine, healing a woman of an issue of blood, and raising Jairus' daughter from death (Lc8); Luke describes how Jesus sent out the Twelve, His feeding the five thousand, and of Peter's testimony Thou art "The Christ of God;" we read of the transfiguration, of healing and teaching (Lc9); of calling and empowering and instructing the seventy, of more preaching and healing, of his teaching that those who receive his disciples receive Him; we are given to know that The Father is revealed by The Son, and we receive the incomparable parable of the good Samaritan (Lc10); we are taught the Lord's prayer, his discourse on casting out devils, his witness that he is greater than Jonah and Solomon, and we hear his chastisement of the Pharisees wherein he states that the blood of the righteous [Zacharias and John the Beloved and the Savior and others] shall be required of that evil generation (Lc11); we are taught to beware hypocrisy, to lay up treasures in heaven, to prepare for His coming; we are taught where much is given, much is required, and we have reminded to us the sobering fact that the gospel causes division in families and among peoples (Lc12); we are taught the need to repent or perish, the parable of the barren fig tree; we learn of healing a woman on the Sabbath, that the kingdom of God is likened to a mustard seed, whether few or many are saved, and we hear His lament over Jerusalem (Lc13); Luke tells us of Jesus' healing on the Sabbath, of humility, of the parable of the great supper, of how those who follow him must forsake all else (Lc14); we learn the parables of the lost sheep, piece of silver, and prodigal son (Lc15); we are taught the parable of the unjust steward, the call to service, condemnation of divorce, and the parable of the rich man and Lazarus (Lc16); we learn of offenses, forgiveness and faith, of the fact that even the faithful are unprofitable servants, of healing of ten lepers, and we are given Christ's discourse on the Second Coming (Lc17); we read the parables of the unjust judge, and of the Pharisee and publican; we are touched by his invitation to little children to come unto him; we are taught how to gain eternal life, of his coming death and resurrection, and we see him give sight to a blind man (Lc18); we learn that his mission is to save souls, the parable of the pounds, riding triumphant into Jerusalem, weeping over Jerusalem, and cleansing the temple for the second time (Lc19); we learn of the Chief priests and their opposition to Jesus, the parable of the wicked husbandmen, of rendering to Caesar what is Caesar's and to God what belongs to God, and the law of marriage (Lc20); Luke recounts the Savior's prophesy of the destruction of the temple and Jerusalem, of signs preceding his Second Coming, and of the parable of the fig tree (Lc21); Luke tells us how Jesus instituted the sacrament, suffered in Gethsemane, was betrayed and arrested, of Peter's denial, of how He was smitten and mocked (Lc22); we read of Christ before Pilate, then before Herod, then before Pilate, and of Barabbas' release; we learn of Christ's crucifixion between two thieves, and of His burial in Joseph of Arimathaea's tomb (Lc23); we learn about angels announcing his resurrection, of Emmaus road, of his appearance and his body of flesh and bones, of his eating food as demonstration that he lives and is resurrected; we hear the Savior's testimony of His divinity and promise of The Holy Ghost; and we learn of His ascension into heaven. (Lc24) (New Testament King James Version, LDSV)

John

John the Beloved in his Gospel of John adds a fourth witness that Jesus is the Christ and that He lives!

"Written by John the Apostle. In John 20:321 he tells us his object in writing is to testify (1) that Jesus is the Christ, i.e., the Messiah, and (2) that Jesus is the Son of God. The scenes from Jesus' life that he describes are carefully selected and arranged with this object in view. The record begins with a statement of Christ's status in the pre-mortal existence: he was with God, he was God, and he was the creator of all things. Finally he was born in the flesh as the Only Begotten Son of the Father. John traces the course of Jesus' ministry, greatly emphasizing his divinity and his resurrection from the dead and citing miracles and sermons to develop his points. He clearly affirms that Jesus is the Son of God, attested to by miracles, by witnesses, by the prophets, and by Christ's own voice. John teaches by contrast, using such terms as light and darkness, truth and error, good and evil, God and the devil. Perhaps in no other record are the holiness of Jesus and the perfidy of the Jewish rulers so plainly declared. This Gospel is supplementary to the other three. It deals mainly with the Judaean ministry, whereas the Synoptists write chiefly of the ministry in Galilee. Several items from this Gospel have been clarified by latter-day revelation, such as D&C 7 and D&C 88:141. (LDS Scriptures, Bible Dictionary, pp. 715-716)

"John testifies that Jesus Christ is the Word of God, the Great Creator who created all things, that He was made flesh and lived among us; John tells of John the Baptist's baptism of Jesus and of John's testimony that Jesus is the Lamb of God; of our Savior's calling of John, Andrew, Simon, Philip, and of Nathanael who said: Rabbi, thou art the Son of God; thou art the King of Israel,: of their believing in Christ (John chapter 1); of turning water into wine in Cana, of attending the Passover, and of cleansing the temple, of how Jesus foretold his death and resurrection, and performed miracles (Jc2); of His telling Nicodemus that a man must be born again of water and of the spirit; of the fact that God so loved the world that he gave His Only Begotten Son to save His children, John recounts John the Baptist's testimony that we who believe on the Son have everlasting life (Jc3); we read of Jesus' teaching a woman of Samaria, of the requirement that we worship the Father in spirit and truth; of eternal life as the reward to those who perform missionary work and harvest souls, how many of the Samaritans believed he is The Messiah; of Jesus' healing a nobleman's son (Jc4); we learn how he healed an invalid on the Sabbath, why men must honor the Son, and Jesus' promise to take the gospel to the dead in the spirit world; we learn of the resurrection, judgment, and assignment to men to glory by the Son; of Jesus' obedience to the divine law of witnesses (Jc5); of Jesus' feeding the five thousand, walking on the sea, and of his testimony that He is the living manna sent from God the Father; we are taught that Salvation is gained by eating the living bread, of how men eat the flesh and drink the blood of Jesus, of Peter testifying that Jesus is the Messiah (Jc6); we learn of refusal on the part of Jesus' kinsmen to believe him, of his teaching his Father's doctrine and of his proclamation of his divine Sonship, that the truthfulness of the gospel is to be known only through obedience, of his offer of living water to all men, and of the divers opinions concerning him (Jc7); we are taught about the woman taken in adultery, the fact that Christ is the light of the world, his proclamation that he is the Messiah, and that true children of Abraham believe in Christ, that He is Jehovah, and "Before Abraham was I Jehovah." (Jc8); we learn how he healed a man born blind on the Sabbath, of Jews accusing him of Sabbath violation, of his lecture to them on spiritual blindness (Jc9); we come to know he is the good Shepherd, that he gained power over death from his Father, that he promises to visit his other sheep, and we hear him again proclaim "I am the Son of God." (Jc10); Jesus bears witness he is the resurrection and the life and Mary and Martha testify of him; He raises Lazarus from the dead; and Caiaphas speaks prophetically of the death of Christ (Jc11); we read of Mary anointing Jesus' feet, of His triumphal entry into Jerusalem, of his foretelling his death, of his teaching that to receive him is to receive the Father (Jc12); John describes Jesus washing the feet of the Twelve, identifying Judas as his betrayer, and commanding his apostles and disciples to love one another (Jc13); Jesus speaks of many mansions, states he is the way, the truth, and the life, and says that to see him is to see the Father. He promises the first and second Comforters (Jc14); John the Beloved testifies that Jesus is the vine and disciples of Jesus are the branches. In the book of John we learn from Jesus the perfect law of love, that his servants have been chosen and ordained by him, and that the world hates and fights true religion. He gives the promise of the Comforter, the Spirit of truth (Jc15); he speaks on the mission of the Holy Ghost, he tells of his death and resurrection, he announces his divine Sonship, and he states that he has overcome the world (Jc16); he offers the great intercessory prayer, is glorified by gaining eternal life, prays for his apostles and all saints, discourses on how The Father and The Son are one (Jc17); Jesus is betrayed and arrested, examined and maltreated before Annas and Caiaphas; Peter denies him; and Jesus is arraigned before Pilate (Jc18); he is scourged and crucified, places his mother in the care of John the Beloved; he dies, his side is pierced with a spear, and he is buried in the tomb of Joseph of Arimathaea. (Jc19); Mary Magdalene, Peter, and John find the tomb empty, he appears to Mary Magdalene, he appears to the disciples, he shows them his resurrected body and Thomas is permitted to feel his wounds. John concludes with Jesus' testimony that He is the

Christ, the Son of God. (Jc20); Jesus appears to the disciples at the sea of Tiberias and says to them: 'Feed my sheep'; He foretells Peter's martyrdom and John's translation. (Jc21).

John the Beloved is also John the Revelator, author of the New Testament Book of Revelation wherein John testifies that he saw the risen Lord. (Revelation 1:9-20)

Book of Mormon twelve disciples and people (Book of Mormon)

Following Christ's Gethsemane experience, death on the cross and resurrection, a multitude gathered on the American continent, "and behold, they saw a Man descending out of heaven; and he was clothed in a white robe; and he came down and stood in the midst of them; .... he stretched forth his hand and spake unto the people, saying: Behold, I am Jesus Christ." (3 Nephi 11:1-10.)

BOOK OF MORMON THIRD NEPHI THE BOOK OF NEPHI CHAPTER 11
CHAPTER 11
[A.D. 34]

1 AND now it came to pass that there were a great multitude gathered together, of the people of Nephi, round about the temple which was in the land Bountiful; and they were marveling and wondering one with another, and were showing one to another the great and marvelous change which had taken place.

2 And they were also conversing about this Jesus Christ, of whom the sign had been given concerning his death.

3 And it came to pass that while they were thus conversing one with another, they heard a voice as if it came out of heaven; and they cast their eyes round about, for they understood not the voice which they heard; and it was not a harsh voice, neither was it a loud voice; nevertheless, and notwithstanding it being a small voice it did pierce them that did hear to the center, insomuch that there was no part of their frame that it did not cause to quake; yea, it did pierce them to the very soul, and did cause their hearts to burn.

4 And it came to pass that again they heard the voice, and they understood it not.

5 And again the third time they did hear the voice, and did open their ears to hear it; and their eyes were towards the sound thereof; and they did look steadfastly towards heaven, from whence the sound came.

6 And behold, the third time they did understand the voice which they heard; and it said unto them:

7 Behold my Beloved Son, in whom I am well pleased, in whom I have glorified my name—hear ye him.

8 And it came to pass, as they understood they cast their eyes up again towards heaven; and behold, they saw a Man descending out of heaven; and he was clothed in a white robe; and he came down and stood in the midst of them; and the eyes of the whole multitude were turned upon him, and they durst not open their mouths, even one to another, and wist not what it meant, for they thought it was an angel that had appeared unto them.

9 And it came to pass that he stretched forth his hand and spake unto the people, saying:

10 Behold, I am Jesus Christ, whom the prophets testified shall come into the world.

11 And behold, I am the light and the life of the world; and I have drunk out of that bitter cup which the Father hath given me, and have glorified the Father in taking upon me the sins of the world, in the which I have suffered the will of the Father in all things from the beginning.

12 And it came to pass that when Jesus had spoken these words the whole multitude fell to the earth; for they remembered that it had been prophesied among them that Christ should show himself unto them after his ascension into heaven.

13 And it came to pass that the Lord spake unto them saying:

14 Arise and come forth unto me, that ye may thrust your hands into my side, and also that ye may feel the prints of the nails in my hands and in my feet, that ye may know that I am the God of Israel, and the God of the whole earth, and have been slain for the sins of the world.

15 And it came to pass that the multitude went forth, and thrust their hands into his side, and did feel the prints of the nails in his hands and in his feet; and this they did do, going forth one by one until they had all gone forth, and did see with their eyes and did feel with their hands, and did know of a surety and did bear record, that it was he, of whom it was written by the prophets, that should come.

16 And when they had all gone forth and had witnessed for themselves, they did cry out with one accord, saying:

17 Hosanna! Blessed be the name of the Most High God! And they did fall down at the feet of Jesus, and did worship him.

Mormon

At age 15, Mormon "was visited of the Lord, and tasted and knew of the goodness of Jesus." (Mormon 1:5-8; 14-15)

BOOK OF MORMON, THE BOOK OF MORMON CHAPTER 1

5 And I, Mormon, being a descendant of Nephi, (and my father's name was Mormon) I remembered the things which Ammaron commanded me.

6 And it came to pass that I, being eleven years old, was carried by my father into the land southward, even to the land of Zarahemla.

7 The whole face of the land had become covered with buildings, and the people were as numerous almost, as it were the sand of the sea.

8 And it came to pass in this year there began to be a war ...

...

14 And there were no gifts from the Lord, and the Holy Ghost did not come upon any, because of their wickedness and unbelief.

15 And I, being fifteen years of age and being somewhat of a sober mind, therefore I was visited of the Lord, and tasted and knew of the goodness of Jesus.

Moroni

"And then shall ye know that I have seen Jesus, and that he hath talked with me face to face ...." (Ether 12:39.)

BOOK OF MORMON, THE BOOK OF ETHER CHAPTER 12

32 And I also remember that thou hast said that thou hast prepared a house for man, yea, even among the mansions of thy Father, in which man might have a more excellent hope;

wherefore man must hope, or he cannot receive an inheritance in the place which thou hast prepared.

33 And again, I remember that thou hast said that thou hast loved the world, even unto the laying down of thy life for the world, that thou mightest take it again to prepare a place for the children of men.

34 And now I know that this love which thou hast had for the children of men is charity; wherefore, except men shall have charity they cannot inherit that place which thou hast prepared in the mansions of thy Father.

35 Wherefore, I know by this thing which thou hast said, that if the Gentiles have not charity, because of our weakness, that thou wilt prove them, and take away their talent, yea, even that which they have received, and give unto them who shall have more abundantly.

36 And it came to pass that I prayed unto the Lord that he would give unto the Gentiles grace, that they might have charity.

37 And it came to pass that the Lord said unto me: If they have not charity it mattereth not unto thee, thou hast been faithful; wherefore, thy garments shall be made clean. And because thou hast seen thy weakness thou shalt be made strong, even unto the sitting down in the place which I have prepared in the mansions of my Father.

38 And now I, Moroni, bid farewell unto the Gentiles, yea, and also unto my brethren whom I love, until we shall meet before the judgment-seat of Christ, where all men shall know that my garments are not spotted with your blood.

39 And then shall ye know that I have seen Jesus, and that he hath talked with me face to face, and that he told me in plain humility, even as a man telleth another in mine own language, concerning these things;

40 And only a few have I written, because of my weakness in writing.

41 And now, I would commend you to seek this Jesus of whom the prophets and apostles have written, that the grace of God the Father, and also the Lord Jesus Christ, and the Holy Ghost, which beareth record of them, may be and abide in you forever. Amen.

Joseph Smith is visited by The Father and The Son

Joseph Smith first saw the Savior in the Sacred Grove at Palmyra, New York. "I saw two Personages, whose brightness and glory defy all description, standing above me in the air. One of them spake unto me, calling me by name and said, pointing to the other — *This is My Beloved Son. Hear Him!" (Joseph Smith 1:1-17)*

PEARL OF GREAT PRICE, JOSEPH SMITH— HISTORY OF JOSEPH SMITH, THE PROPHET *History of the Church*, Vol. 1, Chapters 1-5

1 OWING to the many reports which have been put in circulation by evil-disposed and designing persons, in relation to the rise and progress of the Church of Jesus Christ of Latter-day Saints, all of which have been designed by the authors thereof to militate against its character as a Church and its progress in the world—I have been induced to write this history, to disabuse the public mind, and put all inquirers after truth in possession of the facts, as they have transpired, in relation both to myself and the Church, so far as I have such facts in my possession.

2 In this history I shall present the various events in relation to this Church, in truth and righteousness, as they have transpired, or as they at present exist, being now [1838] the eighth year since the organization of the said Church.

3 I was born in the year of our Lord one thousand eight hundred and five, on the twenty-third day of December, in the town of Sharon, Windsor county, State of Vermont . . . My father, Joseph Smith, Sen., left the State of Vermont, and moved to Palmyra, Ontario (now Wayne) county, in the State of New York, when I was in my tenth year, or thereabouts. In about four years after my father's arrival in Palmyra, he moved with his family into Manchester in the same county of Ontario—

4 His family consisting of eleven souls, namely, my father, Joseph Smith; my mother, Lucy Smith (whose name, previous to her marriage, was Mack, daughter of Solomon Mack); my brothers, Alvin (who died November 19th, 1823, in the 26th year of his age), Hyrum, myself, Samuel Harrison, William, Don Carlos; and my sisters, Sophronia, Catherine, and Lucy.

5 Some time in the second year after our removal to Manchester, there was in the place where we lived an unusual excitement on the subject of religion. It commenced with the Methodists, but soon became general among all the sects in that region of country. Indeed, the whole district of country seemed affected by it, and great multitudes united themselves to the different religious parties, which created no small stir and division amongst the people, some crying, "Lo, here!" and others, "Lo, there!" Some were contending for the Methodist faith, some for the Presbyterian, and some for the Baptist.

6 For, notwithstanding the great love which the converts to these different faiths expressed at the time of their conversion, and the great zeal manifested by the respective clergy, who were active in getting up and promoting this extraordinary scene of religious feeling, in order to have everybody converted, as they were pleased to call it, let them join what sect they pleased; yet when the converts began to file off, some to one party and some to another, it was seen that the seemingly good feelings of both the priests and the converts were more pretended than real; for a scene of great confusion and bad feeling ensued—priest contending against priest, and convert against convert; so that all their good feelings one for another, if they ever had any, were entirely lost in a strife of words and a contest about opinions.

7 I was at this time in my fifteenth year. My father's family was proselyted to the Presbyterian faith, and four of them joined that church, namely, my mother, Lucy; my brothers Hyrum and Samuel Harrison; and my sister Sophronia.

8 During this time of great excitement my mind was called up to serious reflection and great uneasiness; but though my feelings were deep and often poignant, still I kept myself aloof from all these parties, though I attended their several meetings as often as occasion would permit. In process of time my mind became somewhat partial to the Methodist sect, and I felt some desire to be united with them; but so great were the confusion and strife among the different denominations, that it was impossible for a person young as I was, and so unacquainted with men and things, to come to any certain conclusion who was right and who was wrong.

9 My mind at times was greatly excited, the cry and tumult were so great and incessant. The Presbyterians were most decided against the Baptists and Methodists, and used all the powers of both reason and sophistry to prove their errors, or, at least, to make the people think they were in error. On the other hand, the Baptists and Methodists in their turn were equally zealous in endeavoring to establish their own tenets and disprove all others.

10 In the midst of this war of words and tumult of opinions, I often said to myself: What is to be done? Who of all these parties are right; or, are they all wrong together? If any one of them be right, which is it, and how shall I know it?

11 While I was laboring under the extreme difficulties caused by the contests of these parties of religionists, I was one day reading the Epistle of James, first chapter and fifth verse, which reads: *If any of you lack wisdom, let him ask of God, that giveth to all men liberally, and upbraideth not; and it shall be given him.*

12 Never did any passage of scripture come with more power to the heart of man than this did at this time to mine. It seemed to enter with great force into every feeling of my heart. I reflected on it again and again, knowing that if any person needed wisdom from God, I did; for how to act I did not know, and unless I could get more wisdom than I then had, I would never know; for the teachers of religion of the different sects understood the same passages of scripture so differently as to destroy all confidence in settling the question by an appeal to the Bible.

13 At length I came to the conclusion that I must either remain in darkness and confusion, or else I must do as James directs, that is, ask of God. I at length came to the determination to "ask of God," concluding that if he gave wisdom to them that lacked wisdom, and would give liberally, and not upbraid, I might venture.

14 So, in accordance with this, my determination to ask of God, I retired to the woods to make the attempt. It was on the morning of a beautiful, clear day, early in the spring of eighteen hundred and twenty. It was the first time in my life that I had made such an attempt, for amidst all my anxieties I had never as yet made the attempt to pray vocally.

15 After I had retired to the place where I had previously designed to go, having looked around me, and finding myself alone, I kneeled down and began to offer up the desires of my heart to God. I had scarcely done so, when immediately I was seized upon by some power which entirely overcame me, and had such an astonishing influence over me as to bind my tongue so that I could not speak. Thick darkness gathered around me, and it seemed to me for a time as if I were doomed to sudden destruction.

16 But, exerting all my powers to call upon God to deliver me out of the power of this enemy which had seized upon me, and at the very moment when I was ready to sink into despair and abandon myself to destruction—not to an imaginary ruin, but to the power of some actual being from the unseen world, who had such marvelous power as I had never before felt in any being—just at this moment of great alarm, I saw a pillar of light exactly over my head, above the brightness of the sun, which descended gradually until it fell upon me.

17 It no sooner appeared than I found myself delivered from the enemy which held me bound. When the light rested upon me I saw two Personages, whose brightness and glory defy all description, standing above me in the air. One of them spake unto me, calling me by name and said, pointing to the other—*This is My Beloved Son. Hear Him!*

Joseph Smith and Oliver Cowdery see The Great Jehovah, Jesus Christ (Doctrine & Covenants 110:1-10)

DOCTRINE AND COVENANTS OF THE CHURCH OF JESUS CHRIST OF LATTER-DAY SAINTS SECTION 110

1 THE veil was taken from our minds, and the eyes of our understanding were opened.

2 We saw the Lord standing upon the breastwork of the pulpit, before us; and under his feet was a paved work of pure gold, in color like amber.

3 His eyes were as a flame of fire; the hair of his head was white like the pure snow; his countenance shone above the brightness of the sun; and his voice was as the sound of the rushing of great waters, even the voice of Jehovah, saying:

4 I am the first and the last; I am he who liveth, I am he who was slain; I am your advocate with the Father.

5 Behold, your sins are forgiven you; you are clean before me; therefore, lift up your heads and rejoice.

Joseph Smith and Sidney Rigdon see The Father and The Son (Doctrine & Covenants 76:1-24)

THE DOCTRINE AND COVENANTS OF THE CHURCH OF JESUS CHRIST OF LATTER-DAY SAINTS SECTION 76

1 HEAR, O ye heavens, and give ear, O earth, and rejoice ye inhabitants thereof, for the Lord is God, and beside him there is no Savior.

2 Great is his wisdom, marvelous are his ways, and the extent of his doings none can find out.

3 His purposes fail not, neither are there any who can stay his hand.

4 From eternity to eternity he is the same, and his years never fail.

5 For thus saith the Lord—I, the Lord, am merciful and gracious unto those who fear me, and delight to honor those who serve me in righteousness and in truth unto the end.

6 Great shall be their reward and eternal shall be their glory.

7 And to them will I reveal all mysteries, yea, all the hidden mysteries of my kingdom from days of old, and for ages to come, will I make known unto them the good pleasure of my will concerning all things pertaining to my kingdom.

8 Yea, even the wonders of eternity shall they know, and things to come will I show them, even the things of many generations.

9 And their wisdom shall be great, and their understanding reach to heaven; and before them the wisdom of the wise shall perish, and the understanding of the prudent shall come to naught.

10 For by my Spirit will I enlighten them, and by my power will I make known unto them the secrets of my will—yea, even those things which eye has not seen, nor ear heard, nor yet entered into the heart of man.

11 We, Joseph Smith, Jun., and Sidney Rigdon, being in the Spirit on the sixteenth day of February, in the year of our Lord one thousand eight hundred and thirty-two—

12 By the power of the Spirit our eyes were opened and our understandings were enlightened, so as to see and understand the things of God—

13 Even those things which were from the beginning before the world was, which were ordained of the Father, through his Only Begotten Son, who was in the bosom of the Father, even from the beginning;

14 Of whom we bear record; and the record which we bear is the fulness of the gospel of Jesus Christ, who is the Son, whom we saw and with whom we conversed in the heavenly vision.

15 For while we were doing the work of translation, which the Lord had appointed unto us, we came to the twenty-ninth verse of the fifth chapter of John, which was given unto us as follows—

16 Speaking of the resurrection of the dead, concerning those who shall hear the voice of the Son of Man:

17 And shall come forth; they who have done good, in the resurrection of the just; and they who have done evil, in the resurrection of the unjust.

18 Now this caused us to marvel, for it was given unto us of the Spirit.

19 And while we meditated upon these things, the Lord touched the eyes of our understandings and they were opened, and the glory of the Lord shone round about.

20 And we beheld the gory of the Son, on the right hand of the Father, and received of his fulness;

21 And saw the holy angels, and them who are sanctified before his throne, worshiping God, and the Lamb, who worship him forever and ever.

22 And now, after the many testimonies which have been given of him, this is the testimony, last of all, which we give of him: That he lives!

23 For we saw him, even on the right hand of God; and we heard the voice bearing record that he is the Only Begotten of the Father—

24 That by him, and through him, and of him, the worlds are and were created, and the inhabitants thereof are begotten sons and daughters unto God.

Modern Witnesses That Jesus Christ Lives

Apostle Melvin J. Ballard and President Lorenzo Snow (68)
The Living Christ and Living Apostles (69-71)

Apostle Melvin J. Ballard and President Lorenzo Snow: "I think of a beautiful experience of Elder Melvin J. Ballard which occurred while he was serving as a mission president in the northwestern states. He had gone over to the Fort Peck Indian Reservation to take care of mission business. He and his counselors had fasted that they might solve some problems that had come into existence on the reservation. After much fasting and prayer, and after making the best decisions they could, Brother Ballard then got on the train to go back to Portland, Oregon. In the dreams of the night, he found himself in what I would assume to be the Salt Lake Temple. He was in conversation with a group of men. After a period of time an individual came over to him and said that it had been requested of him to go to an adjoining room to meet another individual. Brother Ballard said he opened the door to this adjoining room, and as he looked into the room, he saw seated upon a raised platform the most glorious person he had ever seen. As he entered the room this individual arose and smiled and softly spoke his name. Brother Ballard said that this individual came right up to him and put his arms around him and embraced him and kissed him. Brother Ballard at that moment felt a love so intense that he thought the very marrow of his bones would melt. He said he then fell at the feet of this individual, and, seeing the wounds, he knew he was in the presence of Jesus Christ. Throughout the rest of his life he bore powerful witness to the effect that he would be pleased to give all he had and all he could ever hope to have if he could have the privilege of dwelling in the presence of Christ forever. Brothers and sisters, how that touched my heart.

"I was standing in a beet field on another occasion in Idaho, doing some irrigating. I pulled out of my pocket a crumpled piece of paper and read the account of Lorenzo Snow having the opportunity of being visited by the Master in the Salt Lake Temple. As I read that account, there came to me an assurance that that indeed did occur, that Lorenzo Snow did see the living Christ, that he did converse with him, that he obtained knowledge and power and understanding from him. Again, how my heart was touched with that particular experience.

(George W. Pace, BYU devotional address, July 15, 1975.)

The Living Christ
The Testimony of the Apostles
The Church of Jesus Christ of Latter-day Saints

"The Living Christ: The Testimony of the Apostles, The Church of Jesus Christ of Latter-day Saints," *Ensign*, Apr 2000, 2

As we commemorate the birth of Jesus Christ two millennia ago, we offer our testimony of the reality of His matchless life and the infinite virtue of His great atoning sacrifice. None other has had so profound an influence upon all who have lived and will yet live upon the earth.

He was the Great Jehovah of the Old Testament, the Messiah of the New. Under the direction of His Father, He was the creator of the earth. "All things were made by him; and without him was not any thing made that was made" (John 1:3)). Though sinless, He was baptized to fulfill all righteousness. He "went about doing good" (Acts 10:38), yet was despised for it. His gospel was a message of peace and goodwill. He entreated all to follow His example. He walked the roads of Palestine, healing the sick, causing the blind to see, and raising the dead. He taught the truths of eternity, the reality of our premortal existence, the purpose of our life on earth, and the potential for the sons and daughters of God in the life to come.

He instituted the sacrament as a reminder of His great atoning sacrifice. He was arrested and condemned on spurious charges, convicted to satisfy a mob, and sentenced to die on Calvary's cross. He gave His life to atone for the sins of all mankind. His was a great vicarious gift in behalf of all who would ever live upon the earth.

We solemnly testify that His life, which is central to all human history, neither began in Bethlehem nor concluded on Calvary. He was the Firstborn of the Father, the Only Begotten Son in the flesh, the Redeemer of the world.

He rose from the grave to "become the firstfruits of them that slept" (1 Cor. 15:20). As Risen Lord, He visited among those He had loved in life. He also ministered among His "other sheep" John 10:16) in ancient America. In the modern world, He and His Father appeared to the boy Joseph Smith, ushering in the long-promised "dispensation of the fulness of times" (Eph. 1:10).

Of the Living Christ, the Prophet Joseph wrote: "His eyes were as a flame of fire; the hair of his head was white like the pure snow; his countenance shone above the brightness of the sun; and his voice was as the sound of the rushing of great waters, even the voice of Jehovah, saying:

"I am the first and the last; I am he who liveth, I am he who was slain; I am your advocate with the Father" (D&C 110:3-4).

Of Him the Prophet also declared: "And now, after the many testimonies which have been given of him, this is the testimony, last of all, which we give of him: That he lives!

"For we saw him, even on the right hand of God; and we heard the voice bearing record that he is the Only Begotten of the Father—

"That by him, and through him, and of him, the worlds are and were created, and the inhabitants thereof are begotten sons and daughters unto God" (D&C 76:22-24).

We declare in words of solemnity that His priesthood and His Church have been restored upon the earth—"built upon the foundation of ... apostles and prophets, Jesus Christ himself being the chief corner stone" (Eph. 2:20).

We testify that He will someday return to earth. "And the glory of the Lord shall be revealed, and all flesh shall see it together" (Isa. 40:5). He will rule as King of Kings and reign as Lord of Lords, and every knee shall bend and every tongue shall speak in worship before Him. Each of us will stand to be judged of Him according to our works and the desires of our hearts.

We bear testimony, as His duly ordained Apostles—that Jesus is the Living Christ, the immortal Son of God. He is the great King Immanuel, who stands today on the right hand of His Father. He is the light, the life, and the hope of the world. His way is the path that leads to happiness in this life and eternal life in the world to come. God be thanked for the matchless gift of His divine Son.

THE FIRST PRESIDENCY   THE QUORUM OF THE TWELVE

JANUARY 1, 2000

For teachings and testimonies of the living apostles and prophets, see www.JesusChrist.lds.org "Using the teachings and testimonies of apostles and prophets, JesusChrist.lds.org affirms our faith in the Son of God and the need for all to come unto Him. " (www.lds.org)

Footnote A: Ancient Secular Evidences That Jesus Christ Lived

1. **Josephus, Jewish Historian (72)**
2. **Lucien, Playwright (73)**
3. **Mara Bar-Serapion Letter (74)**
4. **Pliny the Younger, Governor of Bithynia (75)**
5. **Suetonius, Roman Historian (76)**
6. **Tacitus, Roman Historian (77)**

Josephus, Jewish Historian, refers to Jesus in his Antiquities.

Antiquities.18.3.3. Now there was about this time Jesus, a wise man, if it be lawful to call him a man; for he was a doer of wonderful works, a teacher of such men as receive the truth with pleasure. He drew over to him both many of the Jews and many of the Gentiles. He was [the] Christ. And when Pilate, at the suggestion of the principal men amongst us, had condemned him to the cross, (9) those that loved him at the first did not forsake him; for he appeared to them alive again the third day; (10) as the divine prophets had foretold these and ten thousand other wonderful things concerning him. And the tribe of Christians, so named from him, are not extinct at this day. (The Complete Works of Flavius Josephus, Antiquities of the Jews 18:3.3.)

Antiquities 20.9.1. "And now Caesar, upon hearing the death of Festus, sent Albinus into Judea, as procurator. But the king deprived Joseph of the high priesthood, and bestowed the succession to that dignity on the son of Ananus, who was also himself called Ananus. Now the report goes that this eldest Ananus proved a most fortunate man; for he had five sons who had all performed the office of a high priest to God, and who had himself enjoyed that dignity a long time formerly, which had never happened to any other of our high priests. But this younger Ananus, who, as we have told you already, took the high priesthood, was a bold man in his temper, and very insolent; he was also of the sect of the Sadducees, who are very rigid in judging offenders, above all the rest of the Jews, as we have already observed; when, therefore, Ananus was of this disposition, he thought he had now a proper opportunity. Festus was now dead, and Albinus was but upon the road; so he assembled the sanhedrim of judges, and brought before them the brother of Jesus, who was called Christ, whose name was James, and some others; and when he had formed an accusation against them as breakers of the law, he delivered them to be stoned:

but as for those who seemed the most equitable of the citizens, and such as were the most uneasy at the breach of the laws, they disliked what was done; they also sent to the king, desiring him to send to Ananus that he should act so no more, for that what he had already done was not to be justified; nay, some of them went also to meet Albinus, as he was upon his journey from Alexandria, and informed him that it was not lawful for Ananus to assemble a sanhedrim without his consent. Whereupon Albinus complied with what they said, and wrote in anger to Ananus, and threatened that he would bring him to punishment for what he had done; on which king Agrippa took the high priesthood from him, when he had ruled but three months, and made Jesus, the son of Damneus, high priest." (The Complete Works of Flavius Josephus, Antiquities of the Jews 20.9.1)

Lucian, a Playwright and Satirist, refers to Christ in his play.

"Lucian, Satirist and Playwright of the Second Century, wrote a play titled "The Passing of Peregrinus. The hero of the tale, Peregrinus, was a Cynic philosopher who became a Christian, rose in prominence in the Christian community, then returned to Cynicism. Lucian's attack is not so much on Christianity, but on the person of Peregrinus, who took advantage of the Christians' simplicity and gullibility. [Alli.Luc, 99]

"The first quotes tells of Peregrinus, who learned "the wondrous lore of the Christians," became one of their leaders and was revered as a god, lawgiver, and protector, "next after that other, to be sure, whom they (the Christians) still worship, the man who was crucified in Palestine because he introduced this new cult to the world." [Harm.Luc, 13]

"The second quote, regarding these same Christians: "Then, too, their first lawgiver persuaded them that they are all brothers...after they have thrown over and denied the gods of Greece and have done reverence to that crucifed sophist himself and live according to his laws." …

"[T]here is good reason to believe that he would not acknowledge the existence of Jesus if there were any doubt in his mind that Jesus actually existed. He would certainly have satirized Christian belief in a fictional or historically doubtful personage mercilessly, if any such arguments existed at the time.

"Finally, he was in a good position to have known of such issues, being that he moved in the most educated of circles and very likely corresponded and consulted with leading figures of his day.

"In short, Lucian was a person who was "in a position to know" whether or not Jesus had genuine historical roots, and was exactly the sort who would raise any relevant doubts in order to enhance the impact of his satire.

"What do we learn about Jesus and or Christianity from Lucian?

1. Jesus is regarded as founder of Christianity. … Lucian identifies Jesus as being associated with the teachings of Christianity - not with Cynicism!
2. Lucian confirms the method and place of Jesus' execution.
3. Lucian writes about the attitudes and practices of Christians in his time, and about the corresponding attitude of pagans like Lucian towards Jesus and the Christians. Jesus is recognized as a sage and a teacher of some worth; yet Christian belief is generally regarded as absurd.

(Tekton, Education and Apologetics Ministry, Secular References to Jesus: http://www.tektonics.org/jesusexist/lucian.html)

Mara Bar-Serapion letter, Written @ 135 to 165 A.D.

This letter contains the following passage:

"What advantage did the Athenians gain from putting Socrates to death? Famine and plague came upon them as a judgment for their crime. What advantage did the men of Samos gain from burning Pythagoras? In a moment their land was covered with sand. What advantage did the Jews gain from executing their wise King? It was just after that their Kingdom was abolished. God justly avenged these three wise men: the Athenians died of hunger; the Samians were overwhelmed by the sea; the Jews, ruined and driven from their land, live in complete dispersion. But Socrates did not die for good; he lived on in the teaching of Plato. Pythagoras did not die for good; he lived on in the statue of Hera. Nor did the wise King die for good; He lived on in the teaching which He had given."

"How do we know that the Serapion letter does not refer to one of those pretenders? The letter sets out seven distinct criteria describing this Wise King, and none of those pretenders filled all seven descriptions of a person who:

- Was executed;
- Was possessed of wisdom;
- Was executed just before the Jews' kingdom was abolished.

- Was executed before the Jews were dispersed;
- Was executed by the actions of the Jews;
- Lived on in the teaching that he had given;
- Was referred to as a "king."

(Tekton, Education and Apologetics Ministry, Secular References to Jesus: http://www.tektonics.org/jesusexist/serapion.html)

Pliny the Younger, Governor of Bithynia, Writing in @ 106 A.D.

"Pliny the Younger (62?-c.113) was Governor of Bithynia. His correspondence in 106 AD with the emperor Trajan included a report on proceedings against Christians. ... Pliny explained that he forced Christians to "curse Christ, which a genuine Christian cannot be induced to do." He also described their actions and practices thusly:

"They affirmed, however, that the whole of their guilt, or their error, was, that they were in the habit of meeting on a certain fixed day before it was light, when they sang in alternate verse a hymn to Christ as to a god, and bound themselves to a solemn oath, not to any wicked deeds, but never to commit any fraud, theft, adultery, never to falsify their word, not to deny a trust when they should be called upon to deliver it up.

"Pliny directly says he knew nothing UNTIL he was compelled to torture the two deaconesses. This solidly refutes any conjecture that Pliny had prior information.

"This reading is incorrect. After listing those rites that the Christians in question adhered to - meeting on a certain day before light, binding themselves by moral oaths, what looks to be taking the Eucharist - Pliny explains:

"Even this practice, however, they had abandoned after the publication of my edict, by which, according to your orders, I had forbidden political associations. I therefore judged it so much more the necessary to extract the real truth, with the assistance of torture, from two female slaves, who were styled deaconesses: but I could discover nothing more than depraved and excessive superstition.

"What do we learn about Jesus and/or Christianity from this historian/writer? We learn that Jesus was worshipped, and that believers died for belief in Him, in the early second century. ... We learn of several aspects of worship that correspond with the NT: Worshipping on a fixed day, practice of the Eucharist (?), and the ethical grounding of Jesus' teachings.

(Tekton, Education and Apologetics Ministry, Secular References to Jesus: http://www.tektonics.org/jesusexist/pliny.html)

Suetonius, Roman Historian

"Suetonius was a Roman historian and contemporary of Tacitus. Here is the first of the two relevant quotes:

"As the Jews were making constant disturbances at the instigation of Chrestus, he expelled them from Rome.

"A second quote does not mention Jesus, but refers to Christians being persecuted under Nero. ...

"Chrestus," as Suetonius spells it, is the correct Latin form of a true Greek name, so that some would say that it does not refer to Jesus Christ. Benko, for example, has suggested that "Chrestus" was some kind of Jewish agitator who had no association with Christianity, perhaps a semi-Zealot reacting to plans by Caligula to put a statue of Zeus in the Jewish Temple; as for the spelling issue, he points out that Suetonius spells "Christians" correctly, so it is unlikely that he misspelled "Christus." [see Benk.EC49, 410-3] . Some may find support for this in that Suetonius' sentence literally refers to "the instigator," not actually "the instigation." [VanV.JONT, 31, 33; who counters, though, that the name "Chrestus" is otherwise unattested among the Jews. ...

"At worst, the passage reflects Suetonius' confusion after hearing about Jews arguing over a "Chri/estus" who the Christian Jews would have spoken of as still alive. This, and the second passage referring to persecution of Christians, provides us with nothing that we do not find elsewhere or that can be substantially used. Perhaps more important is the possible historical connection with the expulsion of Jews from Rome referred to in Acts (which is commonly dated in 49 AD, though some prefer 41 AD - ...

"If there were Christians in Rome in 41-49 AD, then that's a pretty strong indication that Jesus existed, since His life would have been well within the memories of those living at the time.

(Tekton, Education and Apologetics Ministry, Secular References to Jesus: http://www.tektonics.org/jesusexist/suey.html)

Tacitus, Roman Historian, Writing in the early 2nd century A.D.

"Tacitus'… *Annals* provide us with a single reference to Jesus of considerable value. Rather frustratingly, much of his work has been lost, including a work which covers the years 29-32, where the trial of Jesus would have been had he recorded it. [Meie.MarJ, 89] Here is a full quote of the cite of our concern, from *Annals* 15.44. Jesus and the Christians are mentioned in an account of how the Emperor Nero went after Christians in order to draw attention away from himself after Rome's fire of 64 AD:

"But not all the relief that could come from man, not all the bounties that the prince could bestow, nor all the atonements which could be presented to the gods, availed to relieve Nero from the infamy of being believed to have ordered the conflagration, the fire of Rome. Hence to suppress the rumor, he falsely charged with the guilt, and punished Christians, who were hated for their enormities. Christus, the founder of the name, was put to death by Pontius Pilate, procurator of Judea in the reign of Tiberius: but the pernicious superstition, repressed for a time broke out again, not only through Judea, where the mischief originated, but through the city of Rome also, where all things hideous and shameful from every part of the world find their center and become popular. Accordingly, an arrest was first made of all who pleaded guilty; then, upon their information, an immense multitude was convicted, not so much of the crime of firing the city, as of hatred against mankind.

"What do we learn about Jesus and or Christianity… Tacitus regards "Christus" as the founder of the movement. …He confirms the execution of Jesus under Pilate, during the reign of Tiberius.

1. He indicates that Jesus' death "checked" Christianity for a time. This would hint at the probability that Christianity was recognized to have had some status as a movement (albeit not under the name "Christianity") prior to the death of Jesus.
2. He identifies Judaea as the "source" of the movement. This mitigates against ideas that Christianity was designed piecemeal from pagan religious ideas.
3. He indicates that Christians in Rome in the mid-60s A.D. were dying for their faith. (Tekton, Education and Apologetics Ministry, Secular References to Jesus: http://www.tektonics.org/jesusexist/tacitus.html)

Writer's Comment

We are children of God the Eternal Father with divine potential to become like Him.

He hears and answers our prayers in the name of His Son.

Jesus is the Son.

He is the Christ.

He is the Messiah.

He is the great Jehovah.

He is The Savior of the world.

I share this optimistic view of the future: "Be not afraid!" and "Be of good cheer!" for these are the words of Our Savior and He has overcome the world.

He will soon come again in glory with all His holy angels to rule as King of kings and Lord of lords on this earth.

To your great health, happiness, and prosperity!

I dedicate this small work to you and to my wife and children and grandchildren.

Richard Linford.

P.S. A couple of websites you may find interesting include: www.lds.org and www.mormon.org ; Blog http://jesus-isthechrist.blogspot.com/

Writer's Background

Richard is a Christian – a member of The Church of Jesus Christ of Latter-day Saints. He works at being a good husband, dad, grandpa, and neighbor. He is a Salt Lake Temple worker and former lay bishop and stake presidency member and region welfare services specialist. He was a missionary to the Netherlands for three years and to the Salt Lake City Inner City for seven years. He served as state chairman of The National Conference of Christians and Jews and on the NCCJ national board for many years and on the boards of the National Heart Association, Junior Achievement, and he served as multi-county chairman of the Red Cross. He is a businessman, attorney at law, broadcaster, and has served as CEO of several companies. He is a writer, oil painter, and 'wannabe" golfer.

Several of his published books sold world-wide by <u>www.amazon.com</u> are:

*(Marriage Enrichment) 199 Ways To Make Your Good Marriage Great or Your Bad Marriage Better

*(Christian Hereafter) Andrew Chipman's Christmas Angel

*(Business Turnaround in Economically Trying Times) Stop Strolling Around Naked in Your Business Empire Like 'Alittle Kingly'

*(Light and Darkness; Good and Evil; Life in Perspective) The Young Marine and The Snow – an allegory

*(Christian Conduct) Would Jesus Christ Do That? is the first question!

*(Jesus Christ Lives!) The Jesus Christ Papers, Volume 1, The Many Witnesses that "he lives!"

199 WAYS TO MAKE YOUR GOOD MARRIAGE GREAT OR YOUR BAD MARRIAGE BETTER

ROMANCE AND IMPROVE YOUR MARRIAGE TODAY

RICHARD W. LINFORD

21. COMPLIMENTING ... BECAUSE HONEST, FAIR, KIND COMPLIMENTS EVERY DAY ARE ENDEARING ... BECAUSE WORDS OF APPROVAL ARE WORDS OF LOVE ... BECAUSE YOU CAN COMPLIMENT YOUR SPOUSE VERBALLY OR BY EMAIL OR BY CARD ... BECAUSE BY COMPLIMENTING YOUR SPOUSE YOU HELP LIFT HER OR HIM TO HIGHER, BETTER, MORE CAPABLE LEVELS ... BECAUSE THE WORLD IS HARSH AND YOUR APPROVAL AND COMPLIMENTS MINIMIZE FEAR, FRUSTRATION AND ANXIETY.

22. CONCERTS ... BECAUSE THE SYMPHONY, A ROCK AND ROLL BAND, A YOUTUBE DATE TO WATCH FAVORITES PROVIDES COMMON, MEMORABLE MUSICAL EXPERIENCES THAT BIND YOU TOGETHER.

23. CONFIDENCE ... BECAUSE MOST EVERYTHING CAN WORK OUT ALL RIGHT IF YOU TRUST. BE WORTHY OF THE CONFIDENCE PLACED IN YOU BY YOUR SPOUSE.

24. CONTRIBUTING TO YOUR SPOUSE'S EMOTIONAL BANK ACCOUNT ... BECAUSE DAILY DEPOSITS TO YOUR SPOUSE'S EMOTIONAL WELL-BEING HELP BUILD BALANCES SUFFICIENT TO SUPPORT WITHDRAWALS.

25. CONTROLLING HOW YOU ARGUE ... BECAUSE SETTING GROUND RULES ABOUT HOW YOU ARGUE, HELPS TO ENSURE THAT YOUR ARGUMENTS WILL NOT BE CRITICAL, DIVISIVE, OR HURTFUL ... BECAUSE EACH PERSON SHOULD HAVE OPPORTUNITY TO STATE HIS POINT OF VIEW IN A PEACEFUL, CALM SETTING ... BECAUSE REASONING TOGETHER IS SO MUCH BETTER THAN ARGUING.

Barcode Area

We will add the barcode for you.

Made with Cover Creator

Sold world-wide by www.amazon.com.

Andrew Chipman's
Christmas Angel

Richard W. Linford

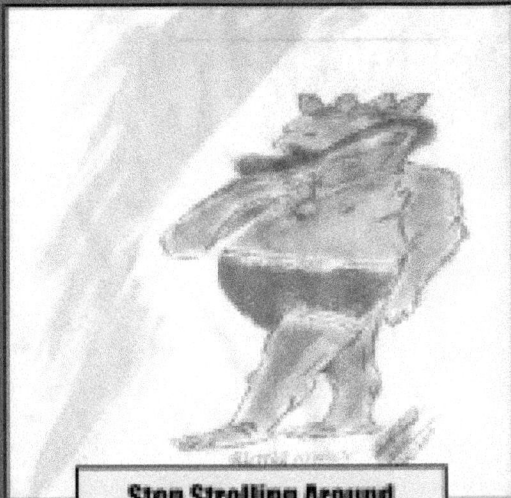

Stop Strolling Around
Naked In Your Business
Empire Like "A Little Kingly"

Put on your business
turnaround threads in
the next 24 HOURS

Richard W. Linford

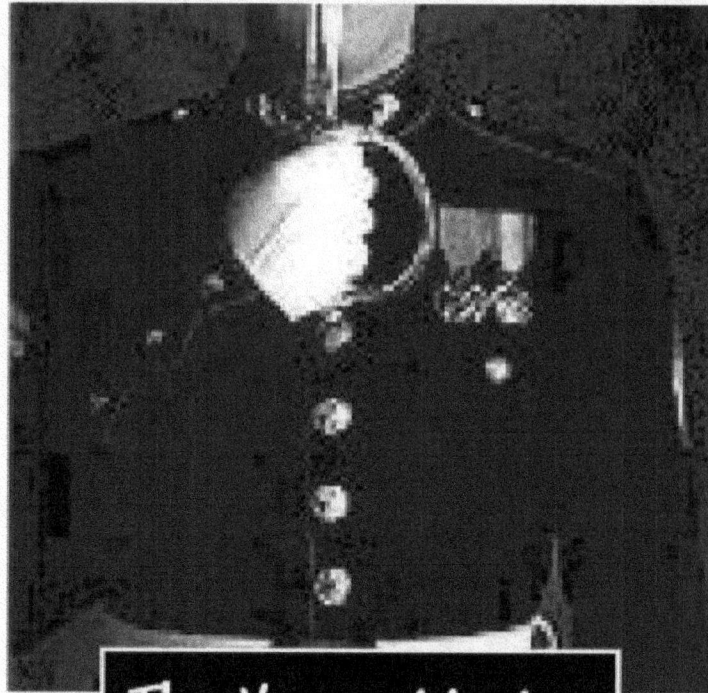

The Young Marine and the Snow

an allegory

Richard W. Linford

"Jesus Christ is King of Kings, Lord of Lords, and Savior of the World. He will soon return to usher in His great Millennial reign of peace, prosperity and love!" *Richard Linford*

* "Would Jesus Christ Do That? is the first question!" "What Would Jesus Do?" is the second question! -- a fiction short story.

* The New Testament Gospel of John with the words of Jesus Christ in bold -- non-fiction.

* Several author's notes you may find of great interest and perhaps even invaluable.

The author is a Christian -- a member of The Church of Jesus Christ of Latter-day Saints (the Mormons), family man, a bishop, attorney at law, businessman, and former state chairman and national board member of The NCCJ -- National Conference of Christians, Jews [and Muslims], a writer, artist and sometime golfer.

Barcode Area
We will add the barcode for you.
Made with Cover Creator

Would Jesus Christ Do That? is the first question!

What Would Jesus Do? is the second question!

Richard W Linford

Sold world-wide by <u>www.amazon.com</u>.

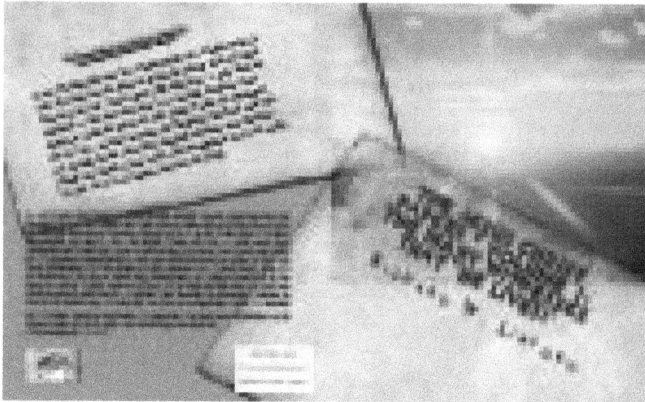

The Jesus Christ Papers

Volume 1

The Many Witnesses that "He lives!"

Richard W. Linford